Thrown on Life's Surge

Bernadette M Redmond

©Bernadette M Redmond

All Rights are asserted by Bernadette M Redmond in accordance with the Copyright, Design and Patents Act 1988.

ISBN-13: 978-1492107156

ISBN-10: 1492107158

Dedicated to Bridgie Duggan-Glynn who took the long road

1934-2011

Table of Contents

1956

January   CH01 - CH15

February   CH16 - CH 21

March   CH22 - CH22

April   CH23 - CH25

May   CH26 - CH27

June   CH28 - CH29

July   CH30 – CH31

August   CH32 – CH37

September   CH38 – CH40

October   CH41 – CH32

November   CH43 – CH46

December   CH 47- CH 52

Chapter 1

With the chimes of the New Year of 1956 a little more than nine hours old Christy Clinton drove at a stately pace across the City on New Year's morning to the leafy south Dublin suburb of Ranlagh with its tree lined streets and grand Victorian mansions and lesser statused Edwardian villas. Turning down Northbrook Road on that bleak January morning I pointed out to him the Hospital on one side of the road with the Nurses Home opposite. His wife, my Aunt Sheila had come along out of a burning curiosity to have a look around. This was well cloaked as concern for my welfare on leaving home for the first time. While he grappled with my suitcase, Sheila, dressed and primped to the nines, sailed up the front steps of a big semi-detached Victorian residence with me at her heels. The door bell was answered by a young girl in a blue serge dress who bobbed at Sheila and bypassing the front room to the right, showed us into a parlour overlooking a substantial lawned garden. A small consumptive looking elderly nun entered before we even had time to sit down. She looked overwhelmed by the Daughter of Charity of St. Vincent de Paul long blue woollen wide sleeved habit, and its soaring seagull type head dress. However, frail as she looked she had Christy and Sheila on their way home within five minutes just giving Christy enough time to transfer two folded pound notes into my hand as he winked goodbye.

Such was my meeting with Sr. Agnes who was in charge of housekeeping as well as the hospital sewing room and laundry. The latter task was not as burdensome as it might seem since the bulk of the washing and ironing was farmed out to the penitents at the nearest Magdalene Laundry in Donnybrook.

'I have arranged for Nurse Donovan to be your guide for the next few days'. 'She will be here soon' she said gesturing for me to follow her up the grand staircase to a first floor bedroom overlooking the tree lined road.

I lugged my suitcase up the stairs bumping it several times which elicited a couple of winces from Sr. Agnes but no reprimand. The room looked like a small ward with a bed in each corner. It smelt of sweaty shoes. A Holy picture graced each wall as well as a notice which read. 'It is forbidden to eat or store food in bedrooms. It attracts vermin'. There were curtains on a track that completely surrounded each bed. 'For modesty' explained Sr. Agnes. I was thinking more of privacy myself. All the curtains were neatly pulled back 'And are only to be pulled if you are undressing or going to bed' she said. Besides a bed each of the four occupants has a chest of drawers, a chair, small wardrobe and attached to the wall a wooden rack with five pegs. From three of the sets of pegs a variety objects hung but before I could scrutinise them Sr. Agnes explained 'They are for your towel, sponge bag, shoe cleaning kit, dressing gown and personal laundry bag'. 'They are most certainly *not* for drying your stockings' she said emphatically, glancing at the rack behind me on which hung four long black offenders 'You will find a small drying room in the basement and a Dutch airer in the bathroom she went on 'And there are sufficient hangers in your wardrobe and space in your drawers for all your possessions so there is no excuse for untidiness.

For several minutes I'd being saying 'Yes, Sister' 'Yes, Sister' like a demented mynah bird. She suddenly stopped talking and looked at me until she had my full attention.
'You've not been away from home before' she half stated, half asked in a kindly tone.

'No, Sister' I responded somewhat puzzled.

'Well Nurse, in time you'll find that while some would say that cleanliness is next to Godliness when you live communally tidiness is equally important. It shows consideration for those who have to clean up after you'.

Most of what she had said I had somehow absorbed, but rational thought has ceased when she called me Nurse. Reality set in. On the foot of the bed in the left hand corner away from the window was a stack of neatly folded uniform and on top was a large folded blue and white striped drawstring bag made from the same material as the dresses, and clearly marked Nurse B M Redmond.

'Let me go through your uniform with you, before I leave you to Nurse Donovan' she said going over to the pile.

She made an inventory checking that everything had been brought across from her domain in the hospital sewing room.

4 dresses
6 starched collars
2 white grosgrain belts
8 starched aprons
2 starched caps
Navy cloak
Small box with studs, safety pins, and hooks and eyes

I had been pre fitted for the uniform at interview so in theory it should fit me. Sr. Agnes left me with instructions to sew name tapes on to all uniform items before sending them to be laundered, and to unpack and bring my case to the basement Trunk Room where it would be locked away. Theresa Donovan later told me caustically 'They don't want you keeping it under the bed in case you do a midnight flit'. I was more charitable and believed it was to make life easier for the cleaner who had to buff our lino covered floors.

~ Prologue DECEMBER 1955 ~

Chapter 2

'What on earth are cash name tapes'? Gran had asked a couple of weeks previously, squinting at a list held at arm's length. Annie Lawlor our next-door neighbour concentrating on extracting a pinch of snuff from her little silver snuff box ignored the question. She sat rubbing the top of the box with her thumb as if trying to remove its fox and hounds engraving while Gran moved the sheet of paper backwards and forwards to bring it into focus. Sheila, Gran's thirty four year old daughter, leaned across the table pinpointing the item.
'They're Cash's name tapes for sewing on clothes' she told her.
'Why does she need fifty' said the ever thrifty Gran ignoring me, her eldest granddaughter sitting across the table from her. Looking at 'The List' I could see the point of her query.
'My uniform will probably have to have them sewn on as well' I contributed.
Attached to the list was a small information leaflet advertising suppliers of the said woven name tapes which I picked up to read. The choice of font was impressive and the thread of the woven name came in several colours. It took me some time to reach the essential information about quantities and price. I can't remember how much they cost but I do remember that the labels came in lots of thirty six and seventy two and seventy two was twice the price. Would the Gran notice? Was the Pope Catholic?

The list in question was my 'trousseau' or the clothing requirements I was expected to possess to train at St Anne's Skin and Cancer Hospital as a Probationer Nurse. I had just been accepted there to complete a year's pre nursing course that would enhance my chances of being accepted for General Nurse

Training. It was mid December 1955 and we were sitting at my grandmothers table in the Artisans Dwellings in Summerhill a tenement rich inner city area in north Dublin. The Dwellings sat facing a row of open doored crumbling Georgian tenements in Upper Buckingham Street but, as their name suggested, they housed artisans, were owned by the Dublin Artisans Dwelling Company and were rented out to families who could guarantee the payment of the weekly rent. I lived with my grandmother and Aunt Tess in No. 31 on the first floor. The Gran, aged 75 and a widow for six years was a little whippet of a woman, too impatient to wear glasses so managed newspaper size print with the aid of a small magnifying glass. On this occasion, and a daily occurrence, the magnifying glass had been misplaced; usually it was recovered from down her bosom to be hauled out on a piece of string.

Across the table was firkin shaped Annie Lawlor, from No. 32, age eighty two, as sallow and brown eyed as somebody born on foreign soil, clad in black, and a neighbour of more than thirty years. She had been a friend of my grandmother all of that time, but since the death of her husband Jim, who made her a widow shortly before my Gran, they had become more supportive of each other. Annie regarded herself as the concierge of our four flat landing's communal hall. Her failing eyesight prevented her from perusing 'The List' but wasn't going to prevent her putting her tu'pence worth in. Sheila was over by the range toasting bread against the stoked red coals. Married for more than a decade she was keeping an eye on the time to get back to nearby Ballybough before her two children got home from school.

I, two weeks into my seventeenth year, sat impatiently at the table waiting for the discussion to reach the dreaded word, *'shopping'*. Shopping with Julia Redmond aka 'the Gran' had been a mortifying and character forming experience since I had come to live with her at the age of eight. Her bargain hunting, frugal and parsimonious ways were bad enough, but when she would refute the prices asked for the provisions on offer by Parnell and Moore Street dealers and local shop keepers I would cringe with embarrassment. Department store shopping was even worse because she would denigrate their stock to sales assistants and floor walkers alike. I would try to pretend I didn't know her from Adam but the ploy never succeeded because if I didn't answer her summons to come and carry the goods purchased she would send the floor walker looking for me, Thank God they didn't have Tannoys in shops in those days, it was bad enough hearing 'Bernie Redmond' repeated enquiringly around the shop as I hid behind racks of frocks. For years I couldn't go in to Boyer's Cassidy's or Collette Modes for fear the floor walkers or sales assistants would recognise me. Gran had been a seamstress in her youth so knew all about the quality and the warp and weft of cloth, matching up patterns and shoddy finishing. She was a customer to be reckoned with and they knew it. ' Well we're going to have to dig deep to get you kitted out' said Gran, making me feel ashamed. I knew it was an expense she could do without and I also know that she would get little help from my father who had a new wife and baby.

'There's one thing for sure' said Annie Lawlor, sucking a Palma Violet, 'We'll send you off to that Nurses Home as well dressed as any farmer's daughter'.

'With 'the pull' youze need to get in I bet yiz'll be the only Jackeen there'.

How true. How true. Annie's only daughter, May had died a few weeks short of her twenty first birthday so she had always treated me like a proxy granddaughter, or a 'poxy' one when I was young enough to draw 'beds' with chalk on the scrubbed landing floor to while away a wet day.

Chapter 3

The List had arrived by the morning post accompanied by a letter accepting me for training, subject to a satisfactory medical and dental examination, and informing me I was to present myself at the Nurses Home in Northbrook Road at 10.00 a.m. on New Year's Day 1956. The letter also stipulated that I would be expected to have in my possession the following items. For those of you with a burning desire to know what was on the List, or have a purulent interest in a young lady's underwear read on, the rest of you skim through it'.

List of requirements
One lockable suitcase or small trunk capable of holding the following;
2 modest dresses (suitable for church or social occasions)
2 below knee plain skirts
2 blouses summer wear
2 long sleeved navy woollen cardigans
1 warm dressing gown
2 long cotton nightdresses or 2 pr cotton pyjamas
2 long sleeved jumpers
1 pair brown court shoes
2 pair black lace up shoes (Nurses range)
1 pair slippers
Shoe cleaning kit in drawstring bag
Toiletries in drawstring bag to include nail brush and scissors
Clearly marked drawstring laundry bag for personal laundry
Basic sewing kit with black / white / mid blue cotton reels.
3 liberty bodices or 3 well fitting white cotton brassieres
3 white cotton vests
3 pair of white cotton knickers
3 white cotton full length slips.

2 roll-on type corsets or 2 suspender belts
6 cotton handkerchiefs
1 sanitary belt
1 box Dr Whites
Hot water bottle
White hair grips and collar studs
Fob watch with second hand
Pair of round ended surgical scissors
Pearce's Medical and Nursing Dictionary
Note pad.
4 exercise books and a selection of pens
50 Cash's name tapes
NB All personal clothing to have nametape sewn in.
Spare name tapes to be given to sewing room on arrival.

In today's materialist world this basic list would seem modest, but in a home of make do and mend to have three of anything would have been deemed the wildest extravagance.
'Holy Muddah a' God' said Annie, 'Youze would tink yiz woz entering a bloody noviciate'.

The same thought had crossed my mind. The Hospital was run by the Daughters of Charity of St. Vincent de Paul and my 'pull' for acceptance had been glowing references extolling my exemplary conduct and character written by Sr. Francis and Sr. Kevin from my school days in North William St. run by the same Order. I knew from my interview that my less than salubrious address and Dublin working class background hadn't gone down well, and looking at the other candidates I could understand why; they were well fed tenant farmers daughters, beef to the heel like Mullingar heifers, with references from their local doctor or

Parish Priest and who already probably had trunks full of clothes from their boarding school days.

'You'd better go over to the Convent and let them know you've got in' said Sheila referring to Sr. Francis, and Sr.Kevin.

'Take this with you' she said, folding the list and putting it back in the envelope careful not to smudge her newly lacquered nails. 'You never know, they might be able to do something'.

Standing up to adjust her hat in the mirror over the range and re-apply her Miner's Strawberry Crush lipstick, she went on 'Christy has contributed enough to their Orphanage over the years to have clothed a dozen children'.

Poor Christy, her husband, was a well known 'soft touch' and much to Sheila's annoyance used to charge up old peoples dry batteries free. Since battery charging was the bulk of his electrical repair business the proceeds were meant to cover the rent on his little shop on Summerhill.

'Sure the poor aul wans don't have two ha'pence to rub together' he would tell an irate Sheila.

'Well those self same 'aul wans' are sitting over in Cleary's snug this minute knocking back glasses of stout' an enraged Sheila would retort totting up the weeks takings.

Chapter 4

The door of the convent attached to North William Street School was opened by a girl a little younger than me, one of the 'boarders' from the attached Orphanage. I recognised her from my sister's class at school but to my shame I couldn't remember her name. 'It's Breege' she reminded me shyly showing me into the panelled statue laden, visitor's parlour. Sr. Francis, who had taught me for five year glided silently into the room pink with delight.
'We've just heard the good news' she beamed.' Aren't you the great girl altogether' she said pumping my hand.
We heard Sr. Kevin before we saw her. She had taught in the boy's school, but I had been in her choir from the age of ten. Rattling of wooden beads, swirling skirt and then her head with its swooping seagull head gear was poked around the open door.
'Well, Bernie Redmond, you've done us proud' she exalted clutching me to her starched bosom. 'That'll be a great smack in the eye for our house in Cork' she said committing a sin against charity.
Question followed question; who had interviewed me? Exchange of looks noted. What was the competition like? When did I start? What did I need? The latter was an invitation to produce The List. They poured over it and seemed unfazed by its contents. They talked together quietly and told me to follow them to the Orphanage sewing room where they measured me from head to toe, telling me they would supply the underwear, black stockings and skirts.
Armed with these good tidings I returned home to find the news of my acceptance had spread around the Dwellings. By the

following afternoon everybody in the block had read the letter, and examined the list with much sucking of teeth and exclamations of incredulity.

'Tree pairs of feckin shoes' noted the turbaned Irene Fitz in amazement as she read the list to Lena Breslin and May Grant, who with Annie Lawlor were sitting drinking tea around Grans table.

'Jazzis Bernie, do dey tink yiz have won the Irish Sweep or wah'? Irene screeched.

'Do dey have to be nu' Lena pondered. 'We could go up de Hill' and have a look' she said putting the suggestion to the Gran.

I knew that Gran was not averse to combing nearby Cumberland Street second-hand street market for bargains. Known locally as 'the Hill' it was a Mecca for the poor, but I also knew that Gran would never contemplate second-hand shoes because penny pinching as she was, she was fanatical about well fitted footwear. While she might scrimp on everything else, as children we always had our feet measured for new shoes. The long ago day when I had buried my brother Seán's recently bought Clarke sandals in the sand at Dollymount was a crime never forgiven and cost me a lot of time red raddling the balcony floor and black leading the Brown and Green range.

'If youze get a few of yards of material I'll run her up a couple dresses that would grace the Shelbourne' May offered.

'I'll get the dressin' gown' said Annie.

'I'll get yah the watch' added Lena to be greeted by an instant chorus of 'Not from Mick'.

'Mick the Tick' lived in a basement flat and made his living selling dodgy watches. He went on his rounds of Pubs and street markets adorned with watches from wrist to elbow. This allowed a quick escape when warranted. He made a point of extolling the great quality of the leather straps, guaranteeing satisfaction for a year or your money back. When the watch ceased to work after a few days and you went to Mick for your money back you discovered that it was the strap that was guaranteed not the watch.

The list was getting shorter, and got shorter still when Betty, my young step mother offered to knit the cardigans and jumpers on her new knitting machine. My Christmas present wish list was going to be very functional, but despite all of this I knew that sooner or later I was in for a shopping marathon with the Gran. As she finalised what I still needed it dawned on her that we were going to have to shop before the New Year sales. I saw, and recognised the steely eyed look of determination to take on the floor walkers, the arbiters of what reduction could be made by a sales woman if pushed by a determined enough bargain hunter. As well as being a connoisseur of quality my grandmother was a grand master of bargain hunting. I can tell you retrospectively that after four, 4 hour sessions of plodding from shop to shop everything was bought, and for not a penny more than it would have cost in the sales.

The Gran hummed with satisfaction, I was traumatised for life, as was my brother a few years later when she 'took' him to buy a new suit. Not every eighteen year old young man has the mortifying experience of having his Granny adjust his genitalia to make sure of the fit of the trousers. For the rest of his life he broke into a cold sweat on entering a tailoring establishment, and he only has to see the name 'Burtons' to need reviving in the nearest hostelry.

By New Years Eve my case was full and the list was down to its last few items. North William Street nuns had sent a large parcel via Sheila and had been bountiful in their generosity. Sheila herself bought me a dark green woollen coat, not on the list but much needed. We had gone quietly into Cassidy's and purchased it without fuss. Well, without fuss in the shop, but it was days before the tsking and tutting ceased and words like 'bare faced robbery' faded from every conversation with the Gran. My Aunt Tess bought my fob watch while Lena had given me a good quality second-hand leather shoulder bag, no doubt, bought on the Hill. The only item causing concern was Annie Lawlor's dressing gown. Gaudy salmon pink satin, flimsy in the extreme and totally unsuitable I knew it would be deemed vulgar and common by the maker of The List but I didn't care. Annie could ill afford to buy it and obviously thought it was gorgeous. Also it reminded me of my deceased Ma who had trailed about in a similar gown thinking it the height of sophistication, although totally impractical, in a draughty Georgian house.

~ January 1956 ~
Chapter 5

In the Nurses Home I had just finished packing everything away when I heard voices coming up the stairs, Cork accents preceding them into the room. Two Nurses in full regalia entered and looked me up and down. 'Rumusth be Redmond' the freckled serious looking sturdy one said, stating a fact rather than asking a question. They took off their cloaks and hung them on a peg.
'I'm Luchy the well nourished cheerful black haired one added 'As in L-U-C-E-Y' 'Wedontushe Christian nameshs'.
'Roullbe 'Nurse Redmond' sho or 'Redmond' winwe kinbeoverherd otherwishe roullbe watevir rouwant tobecalled, I'm Dorothy endishbe Theresha so, nodding at her colleague whom I assumed was Theresa Donavan.
'Now exchuse mebutim gointabed' she said pulling her curtains.
'Wake me for dinner sho' she told Donovan.
'What an extraordinary thing to do' I thought.
Donovan reading my face smiled and said
'Roukin niver git enough shleep indis place; roullsoon lirnto shleep sthandinup'.

The Cork and Kerry habit of interchanging 'y' and 'r' was confusing. While they used the plural 'ye' like most culchies in the singular it becomes 'rou' instead of 'you'. They also interjected 'h's' everywhere but particularly after the s and st sounds so that sleep became shleep, and stop became sthop and the ended most sentences with an enquiring 'so'. But worst of all was the way they ran words together without taking a breath. I can't go on writing in this vernacular because it will drive us all mad; just take my word for it that you get used to it.
'Now let's get you into this uniform' she said. I began to strip off my dress and she stood there looking at me in amazement.

'Sweet Jesus', she whispered. 'Will you get behind your curtains' 'you'll give Aggie a heart attack if she comes in' she said trying to keep a straight face.

I was bright red with embarrassment. I had a full length slip on which would have ensured my modesty in a department store changing room, but apparently did not meet Nurses Home standards. The uniform dress of heavy blue and white striped cotton fitted well but was mid calf length rather than the required two inches below the knee.

'You look as if you've had just come out of an orphanage' she groaned.

'No use asking Aggie to take them up she'd be happy if they were tipping the ground and would give you aprons the match' she said bundling up the four dresses.

'Do you have any sweets or biscuits' she asked.

Gran had supplied me with a tin of biscuits which I had hidden illicitly in my wardrobe. Not an hour in the place and I was breaking the rules already. Should I declare the contraband?

'Yes, I confessed,' I've got biscuits'

'Get them out' she commanded.

Picking up the dresses and a packet of custard creams and glancing at her fob watch she grabbed her cloak and looking as if she was in a state of advanced pregnancy zoomed from the room. She left with the injunction that if Aggie appeared I was to conceal the lack of uniform and say she'd had to go over to the hospital for a minute. I suspected it was a cardinal sin to alter uniforms so whatever Donovan was doing was likely to get her into trouble. I sat waiting in trepidation, worrying that I would be sent home in disgrace. It was at this point that I realised I was cold and that there were no radiators in the room, neither were there any wall plugs or looking glasses. On the wall behind each bed head rail was an odd shaped dark patch in exactly the same place. A mirror had not been a requirement on my list so apart from a small pocket mirror I had no means of looking at any other part of me. I suppose vanity being one of the seven deadly sins it was right up there with modesty on Sr. Agnes's list. Dorothy Lucey snored softly away behind her drawn curtains and I envied her the warmth of her bed. The shifts being 7.30 to 8.00 you had three hours off during the day. This could mean a late start or an early finish, or a 10 to 1 or 2 to 5 break. Once a week you had a 10.00 to 1.00 and a half day from 1.00, which apart from being on the ward from 7.30am to 10.00am was the equivalent of a day off. You got an actual day off every second week. I suppose we worked about 56 hours a week because I remember when I started my General Training we only worked 48 and it seemed a doddle.

It felt like eternity before Donovan returned but was probably less than a quarter of an hour. Dresses expertly shortened, and fit to withstand any amount of scrutiny for illicit alteration, were pulled from under her cloak.
'Maggie did them for me' she explained.
'She's in charge of the sewing room'. 'She does me the odd favour and the custard creams got us an express service'.
Dress on, the nursing cap made up to Theresa Donovan's non regulation standard, was perched on my coiled plaited hair in an ornamental fashion and held in place with white hair grips. 'You don't want to be going around lookin' like a half baked eejit, do you' she'd remarked as she fashioned the cap up to less than half its regulation size with cunning folds and pleats, negating its purpose which was to prevent infection to patients by covering my hair. Completely dressed I wanted to see what I looked like so asked about looking glasses. 'Not one in the place' she lamented

but taking me to the top of the stairs she left the bedroom door open behind me and going down to the half landing she pulled the blind on the big window. It was an old blackout blind so with the light from the bedroom streaming behind me a young nurse appeared mirrored on the blind. I couldn't believe how smart and professional I looked. I had knots in my stomach from apprehension as the reality of my undertaking hit me. Supposing a patient thought I was a real nurse, supposing I poisoned or killed somebody? Raising the blind Donovan brought me back to earth
'Well ye'd certainly click if you turned up at a police ball dressed like that'. 'Them Guards can't resist a nurse in uniform' she teased.
'I think it's the black stockings myself' I joked straightening my seams.
All this conversation had taken place with me trying to keep up with Donavan's fast Cork accent and trying not to ask her to repeat too many things.
Uniformed and ready I was set for whatever the day might bring.
'Have you got a note pad' she asked abruptly?
I patted my pocket, withdrew it and we sat on my bed until ten to one with me writing down a list of do's and don'ts, and enough rules and regulations to fill page after page. Waking Lucey we made our way to the dining room for dinner.

Chapter 6

The dining room was in the basement. A large gloomy room it had a sign over the door saying Refectory, two windows looking out on the front of the house with two tables each set with six place settings and jugs of water. Two further unset tables of equal size were pushed against the far wall. Four pair of eyes glanced at us then went on eating. Donovan went to the empty table and gestured for me to sit opposite her. Lucey went to the other to join the four.
'I'll introduce you later' she said, 'they only have half an hour for dinner unless they're off until five' she explained.
She had explained the off duty shifts to me, but they were in my notebook, not yet my head, so I just nodded sagely.
The blue serged door opener, now wearing an apron, appeared with two plates. 'It's Wednesday so it must be sausages' Donovan said in anticipation. Blue Serge put the plates in front of us smiling in knowing response.
'Mary, this is Nurse Redmond' 'She's in O'Driscoll's bed 'Donovan said addressing Blue Serge who smiled silently in acknowledgement and moved on.
'She's our Maid' she explained.
I must have looked surprised.
'Don't go getting any delusions of grandeur she said with her mouth full 'She's a house maid not a ladies maid'.
I looked at the substantial plate of food in front of me and wondered how I would get through such a huge portion. Looking around nobody else was having any difficulty; in fact the others were concentrating fiercely and eating at a great pace. Donovan caught me looking at them.

'Like pigs at a trough you're thinking'.
What a mind reader.
'Well Redmond, this time next week you'll have joined the bonhams because when you only get half an hour for dinner' you either go hungry or learn to gobble your food'.

I hate to admit that she was right. Nurses become fast eaters for life. We make a holy show of ourselves when eating out and at dinner parties. Pudding was a large bowl of jam roly poly and custard. I waited in vain for a cup of tea. Gran always had a fresh pot of tea on the table which was poured at will, before, during and after a meal. At some point I was informed by Sr. Bernardino a nun that I learned to despise that this was a vulgarity practiced by the working classes who knew no better.
Following dinner Donovan took me on a tour of the Nurses Home starting with the rest of the basement.
Trunk Room 'Locked' she said; 'Key with Mary'.
'Drying Room' she droned as we passed a room warmed by some means. 'Don't ever leave stockings in here, and if you're drying anything else make sure you're around to keep an eye open.
'Why' I asked innocently.
'Because somebody will pinch your clothes' she responded.
I couldn't believe that a dozen nurses living under the same roof would steal from each other. Hadn't any of them been taught right from wrong?
'You've not been to boarding school have you' she asked. I shook my head.
'Well you'll find that some people would take the eye out of your head and come back for the eyelashes'
I thought about the people in the Dwellings, some of them dependent on the weekly visit to the Pawn to pay their bills, scraping together a few coppers for the penny dinners across the

road in the Legion of Mary kitchen, or waiting for the pay out of a Providential cheque. They came and went among their neighbours flats, some perhaps envious of others possessions, but I had never experienced one neighbour stealing from another.

'And don't think that because your wardrobe door has a lock it can't be opened' Donovan told me, 'I know my key open yours because O'Driscoll was always losing hers'.

Right, I thought, my possessions were hard come by and *nobody was going to take them from me*. At the first opportunity I must do something about it, and unsightly or not my drying stockings were going to be hanging on my peg board overnight.

The sitting room was the large ground floor front room. It was furnished with a selection of single easy chairs, low tables, and a couple of writing desks, a small table with a crackling radio, two radiators and an unlit, set, open fire. On the over mantle were branches of sad looking holly intertwined with a few Christmas tree baubles. A half life size statue of Mary Immaculate on a plinth gazed at some spot on the ceiling. Holy pictures and the food notice were replicas of the bedroom ones.

'The fire isn't lit before 6.00pm' 'Mary lights it' Donovan explained.

I looked at the statue. 'No, Mary, the maid' she said sarcastically.

Donovan observed me touching a radiator which was giving out a hint of heat.

'Cloaks are not supposed to be worn in here but we'd die of cold in this weather if we took any notice' she said rubbing her hands briskly together. 'Usually nobody bothers us in here, but if one of the nuns come in just slip it off your shoulders and pretend you're just about to hang it up'.

My notepad was filling up rapidly with rules and regulations but I had a terrible forbearing that I was going to be committing sins of omission and commission for some time to come. So far I had filled pages on rules on *when* and *where* to wear cardigans, aprons, and the cloak. Sin of sins would be to go out wearing a uniform dress under my new bottle green coat. By the time we had toured the house I had learned that No.24 housed twelve probationers, the other part of the semi detached No.25 was the Convent where the nuns and Mary and Winnie the maids lived. They were two separate establishments; the only access was through a shared kitchen in the basement.

Chapter 7

Two o'clock found me outside Matrons office by pre appointment. Dress code dictated by Donovan was dress, cap and cloak, the latter to be removed before entering the sanctum. Sr. Mary Joseph, elderly and austere was somebody I wouldn't want to annoy.

'Well Nurse, are you settling in' she inquired.

I was fairly sure she had no interest whatsoever in the answer because her eyes were roving over a document on her desk but I praised Donovan and Sr. Agnes to the skies anyway. I was still standing by her desk having received no invitation to sit down when her eyes x-rayed me from head to toe travelling upwards again to my head.

'Who made up your cap Nurse', she asked stepping forward and unpinning it from my hair.

Lie, or get Donovan into trouble? I suspect she knew the answer so I said nothing. She unfolded Donovan's carefully crafted folds and pleats and handed me back the result which came down to my forehead and partially covered my ears forcing me to bend them forward to accommodate it.

I was now invited to sit as she talked at length about the vocational nature of Nursing, the need for personal discipline, long hours, seemly behaviour, purity of heart and mind, and our duty to provide spiritual as well corporal care to our patients. My acceptance by the hospital was an honour I was told, and I should offer up my duties to God, his Crucified Son and Blessed Mother by performing them to the best of my ability. I also got a lecture on 'Aspirations' which I thought was about what my plans were only to discover she was talking about developing the worthy habit of offering one line prayers to God, Mary and the Heavenly Hosts of Saints as I went about my duties. An instant intersession to St. Jude came to mind but I didn't think I'd get much sympathy since I was standing there of my own free will. A list of do's and don'ts followed which went over my head, primarily, because I was totally unnerved by the tenor of the meeting, but also because I hadn't the gumption to remove the note taking pad from my pocket. My only hope was that Donovan had either told me or intended to tell me. I knew the 'don'ts' included no makeup and no jewellery and the 'do's' involved personal hygiene, hair to be off my face and collar and nails to be unvarnished short and well scrubbed. Deodorant was a must; perfume was verboten.

I didn't know whether to call her Matron, Reverent Mother or Sr. Mary Joseph therefore ended up calling her nothing, so that when she passed me a cloth covered A5 book as it it was the Holy Grail I merely said 'Thank you' which made her look at me as if I has no manners. She explained that it was a Schedule of Training. It already had my name and start date on the fly leaf. I opened it nervously and saw, set out across double lined pages detailed lists of activities with three narrow tick list columns with Observation, Participation, and Proficient written sidewise along the top of the columns. The opposite page had a vertical line dividing a 'Comment' space which took up two thirds of the page, the other third reading 'Signature'. I was responsible for the 'Observation' ticks. Whoever was responsible for my participation would tick the appropriate column but only a Sister could deem me 'Proficient'. The last pages in the Schedule were blank and were to be completed by the Ward Sister in the form of a report at the end of my allocation to her domain. We ended up agreeing how privileged I was to be here before she nodded permission for me to exit her presence. I learned later the Mullingar heifers hadn't made it.

'Jezzis wept Redmond, what happened in there' Donovan could hardly talk with laughing.

'You look like a cretin' she said taking the cap off my head and refolded and pleated it to its unorthodox shape.

'Don't worry, you won't see her for weeks, and she'll never notice anyway' she continued

'She walks around with her eyes on the ground, practicing *'Custody of the Eyes'*.

For those of you who do not know or have long since forgotten, to practise Custody of the Eyes is the duty of a religious, not only because it is necessary for their own improvement in virtue, but also because it is an example for the edification of others.

'Did you get the 'Offer it up speech' she asked?

'Christ Donovan, I hadn't bargained on all this Holy stuff, I'm not sure I even believe in God' I told her.

'I half expected to hear that flagellation was compulsory'.

'I wouldn't worry' she responded with a laugh 'They haven't turned any of us in to nuns yet tho' they're always on the lookout for vocations' but as long as you go to Mass on Sundays and days of obligation they'll leave you alone'.

'You might as well see the Chapel while we're here' she added as we turned down a corridor which had been added at the back of the original building.

The Chapel was a little haven of peace. Donovan pointed out a notice board on the wall containing a list of services and a Liturgical Year calendar. On a small table lay a Book of Remembrance and a rack of pamphlets for sale, with an embedded honesty box in the wall nearby. We nodded at a patient and a visitor sitting in prayer having lit candles in front of the statue of St. Anthony. They would probably have preferred St. Peregrine but there wasn't one to hand.

As we genuflected to leave she said 'It's a great skive if you have to accompany a patient to Benediction,' It gets the weight off your feet for half an hour'. I knew by then that I was going to like Donovan.

Chapter 8

3.30 p.m. and we were back in the dining room for tea. Places were set as for lunch with Mary serving tea from an enormous teapot. Each table had a communal helping of jam and a plate with a mountain of buttered bread, the former would not be replenished the latter would. Checking my notes I knew that the first tea break was 3.00 and that we were in time for the second sitting. Again, there were three probationers at the other table but sitting in different seats. Again, they nodded, smiled and went on eating.
'Do we sit in particular places' I asked?
'Yes, you're sitting in O'Driscoll's place she replied 'So you're stuck opposite me' Donovan devoured several slices of bread taking more than a fair portion of jam
'Well you'd better learn not to eat my share of the jam' I joked.
'No promises' she responded 'but if you want jam you learn to get here on time' she said chewing vigorously.
Over time I noted the only alteration to the tea menu would be the colour of the jam and the fact that we got a scone or a slice of cake on Sundays and Holy Days. I was not hungry but was dying for a cup of tea; I drank until my bladder could hold no more.
Tea over Donovan said 'We're off at five so we'll just have time to show you the layout of the Wards'.
I winced at the thought and the fact that my new shoes were rubbing didn't help. I cursed The List Maker for not having included a box of plasters but once again Donovan came to the rescue with a purloined bottle of mentholated spirit and some plasters. Feet revived we went across to the hospital, this time the dress code stipulated an apron because we would be going on the

Wards and we might get involved in having to do something. My God! Do something? Like what? I was weak with panic.

'Look, she said, as we walked through the front door 'Stay with me (like glue), don't wander off (as if), and don't look at anybody (I would be an instant expert on *Custody of the Eyes*)'.

I felt an urge to cling to the hem of her apron as I became her shadow. My tour of the Wards and private wing was reaching an uneventful climax in St Peters Ward where Donovan was introducing me to a stately but kindly looking nun, Sr. Josephine. This was going to be where my first month would be spent under Donovan's wing.

We were standing in middle of the male six patients Ward when I realised my shadow and Sr. Josephine had vanished.

'Nurse', somebody called.

I knew whoever it was could only be calling me. I pretended to be engrossed in my notepad. Several more 'Nurse' calls followed, each sounding more desperate. Eventually the desperation was spelt out.

'I need a bottle Nurse' a voice wailed.

I knew what he meant and I remembered the sluice room was through the side door of the ward. OK, I thought I can handle this, and went to get a urinal. It never entered my head to pull his curtains to allow him some privacy I just stood by to relieve him of the glass bottle containing the warm amber liquid. I was on my way back to the sluice when behind me a loud outraged voice bellowed

'Nurse'! *What – do – you – think – you – are – doing*' it said emphasising every word through gritted teeth.

The nun, who had interviewed me with Matron and had not been impressed with my Jackeen working class background and tenement ridden neighbourhood, had come gliding up behind me and was practically dancing with rage. She moved with such silent grace that many a time in the next year I was to wonder if she had wheels attached to her feet. She ranted on and on about patient dignity and privacy until Donovan came running apologising on my behalf. When she started on Donovan I realised that nun, or not, this woman was a bully. Her cold gray eyes swivelled back to me and held mine in an effort to humiliate and intimidate me into submission while she continued her rant. The Gran could have told her she was wasting her time 'Youze could hang, draw and quarter that wan, grind her into mince meat and she'd still be spitting back at you from the pan' would have been her expert view which would not have been open to dispute or debate. I held her eyes and she broke contact first. It was a small victory. Sr. Bernardino has no idea how close she came to having a desperate mans bladder full of urine in the face. I learned I should have pulled the curtains and covered the urinal on its way to and from the sluice. Donovan took the offending utensil and disposed of it appropriately. While we washed our hands she heaped cursed on my head. I thought 'Hmm, not a member of the White Star League then'. My good catholic upbringing commended me never to set up as judge of another, but I knew that if St Peter really has a book, and there is a day of reckoning, then that bitch of a nun was never going to heaven.

Chapter 9

6.00 p.m. and we were in the dining room again for the first sitting for supper. I learned the cook and the 'skivvy' lived out and only cooked dinner, so supper was always a cold collation unless soup was involved when either Mary or Winnie were deemed to have enough culinary expertise to reheat it. Tonight was a substantial potato and vegetable soup obviously made from left over's from mid day dinner, but good none the less. No sign of Mary so the soup and bowls were on a side table on a trivet warmed by night lights. A large plate of unbuttered bread was on each set table. We helped ourselves but I had no appetite all I wanted was a cup of tea, but again, there was no tea on offer only glasses for water.
'There'll be an urn of cocoa in here at 8.00' Donovan told me.
Small consolation, I hated cocoa.
We headed for the bed room to observe the evening's dress code. If you were staying in you had to remove your cap and apron and change into slippers. Our lovely warm red lined cloaks must be hung up and a cardigan donned if relaxing in the sitting room. Dressing gowns were at all times to be worn over night clothes. God, was I ever going to get the hang of all this and stay out of trouble? Donovan had the bed across from me by one of the windows. Looking around I realised I had the best bed space in the room. I was in the cosy corner away from the drafts from windows and the door. I wondered why nobody had taken the opportunity to swop, but realised in time that a designated bed space gave you a sense of identity. For weeks the others referred to my niche as O'Driscoll's bed. I only felt fully accepted when it became Redmond's.

Donovan suggested we wash our stockings before settling down for the evening. She showed me how to wring them out in a towel, reshape them and hang them over the pegs.

'Don't worry about Aggie, 'she only ever comes up here on an occasional morning to check that you've made your bed and pulled back your curtains' she promised.

With the fire lit, the radiators struggling to emit a decent amount of heat, the heavy sage green curtains pulled and chairs moved in semi circles around the sources of heat the sitting room felt cosy and warm. By the time everybody had come off duty at 8 o'clock I had met all my fellow probationers. Fast Cork accents predominated. Sheila Brady, Abina Corcoran, Mary Cronin; sisters Mary and Kitty Mc McCarthy, and Dorothy Lucey, whom I had already met were all from Cork and made me welcome. Two more sisters, Patricia and Mary Harbourne, who could pass as Dubliners introduced themselves as being from Co Wicklow. Bernie Carroll's rolled 'r's told me she was Co Tipperary born and bred. She was not related to Rita Carroll a quiet girl from Co Monahan. A familiar accent from childhood holidays identified Philomena Kelly as a resident of Co Galway. I wondered how the name business worked out with sisters and people with the same surname but listening to Bernie Carroll being called 'Tip' Pat Harbourne 'PatHar' or 'Pater' and Kitty Mc McCarthy 'Puss' I assumed there was a way round it. The twelfth probationer known as 'The Suck', was from Co. Meath and had left just before eight to join Sheila Brady on night duty. I learned The Suck was a pet of Sr. Bernardino's and was suspected of carrying tales so was heartily disliked by everybody. Sympathy was expressed for Brady who was unfortunate enough to currently share the night shift with her.

Donavan regaled everybody with my experience with 'Creeping Jesus' or 'C.J.' as Sr. Bernardino was called because of the silence of her approach, and my induction with Matron. I learned that Matron had dual roles so I was to address her as Matron when she was on Duty, Reverent Mother if I met her going about her non hospital duties and never Sr. Mary Joseph. With St. Peters Ward having a right of way from the Wing to the Chapel I could foresee that this going to be a minefield and said so.

'Well, keep out of her feckin way then' Donovan said 'and don't look at her, pretend you're practicing *Custody of the Eyes*'.

Amidst much good humour everybody entertained me with horror stories about run in's with C.J. It seemed that Murphy's Law was well established when it came to ensuring that attainment occurred when no one was looking and disaster when CJ was watching. As far as I was concerned this was to become a way of life. My Karma had been set early in life, possibly even in an earlier life.

'At least ye won't have to go far if you want to make a run for it' Phil Kelly said.

'Too late' Donovan retorted. 'Her case is in the Trunk Room'.

'Give it a go' a Cork voice encouraged, 'Rou'll settle in like the rest of us'.

I would hazard a guess that most of them had the experience of boarding school to fall back on, but this was my first night away from home. However looking at their friendly faces and observing rules being flouted right and left I was immensely cheered. I stopped worrying about Sr. Agnes entering and finding black stockings draped over the fireguard, cloaks being worn by those who had not got a fireside chair, mugs of cocoa everywhere, a packet of biscuits, courtesy of a patient, and sin of sins, Mary Harbourne who had just come from the bathroom wearing only her pyjamas. However by 9.45 the room looked as if we had never used it. Curfew was 10.00 p.m. when one of the nuns came through from next door to lock the front door. Sr. Bernardino was one of the ones who would check the sitting room as well and was not averse to collaring any poor unfortunate in her path, or dragging somebody out of bed to make them tidy it up.

  I had been keeping an eye on the bathroom looking forward to a good soak only to be told by Donovan that baths weren't allowed after 10.00 because of the noise of the geyser. I settled for a wash down and was heartened to learn that there was always instant hot water so most people chose to bathe at leisure during off hours during the day. Having observed the plain serviceable woollen dressing gowns worn by the others I had yet to unveil Annie Lawlor's pink satin creation which was wrapped in tissue paper in my chest of drawers. I said a silent 'Sorry' to Annie. I knew she, and Gran would have spent the day wondering how I was getting on.

Chapter 10

The following morning at 6.45 a.m. we were roused by young Mary putting her head around the door to tell us the time. Donovan and I were on a straight through 7.30 to 5 rota. There were no sounds from behind her curtain so I didn't know whether to wake her or not. I got myself ready and began to get worried that we would be late for breakfast when the room door opened and in she came fresh from the bath. She looked me up and down and said

'Put a lick of polish on dem shoes and put yesterday's apron on.'

I didn't dare tell her it was screwed up in the laundry bag provided by Sr. Agnes. 'We don't change aprons until we come back for morning break' by then all the beds will be made and the dirty jobs done'. She didn't elaborate but I assume she meant bed pan rounds and such like. I tried to work out if I have enough aprons to see me through till laundry day, so while she was behind her screens I took a surreptitious look at my notepad and read

Monday; Uniform laundry to be left by the basement door by 8.00
Returned to your room Thursday pm
Tuesday; Personal laundry to be left in named laundry bag by basement door by 8.00am
Cotton items only will be accepted.
Unnamed items will be kept until claimed.
Wednesdays; Bed linen; one sheet, one pillow case and towel will be exchanged.
Maid will leave replacement sheet, pillow case and towel providing those for exchange are left folded on your chair.
Friday; Personal laundry returned to your room pm.

My ability to do a simple calculation deserted me so I donned a newly starched apron anyway hoping Donovan wouldn't notice. I hoped in vain, but she just rolled her eyes. Sharing our room were

Abina Corcoran as well as Dorothy Lucey who were obviously on the 1 to 8 shift so were having a sleep in.

Mary ticked our names off her list as we entered the Dining Room and noted our time of arrival. While Mary wouldn't want to get anybody into trouble she had to be accurate in case Sr. Agnes came in to check. Breakfast was served from 7.00 but you were expected to be seated by 7.10 which gave you about ten minutes to present yourself on the Ward by 7.20. Missing breakfast was not tolerated. The porridge was keeping warm on the trivet and plates of brown soda bread and dishes with pats of butter in separate glass dishes were on the table. The porridge was surprisingly good served with cold creamy milk.
'Why don't they butter the bread' I asked.
'Stale brown bread goes into the pig feed so the butter would be wasted, left over white bread and butter becomes bread and butter pudding' she explained.
'Come on she said, let's go'.
I hadn't yet learned to talk and eat at the same time so was only finishing my porridge, and hadn't even had a sip of my tea.
'Don't worry about the bloody 'tay' she said ignoring my plaintive cry.
'*Offer it up*' she smirked, imitating Matrons piety.
A childhood memory came to mind as I donned my cape and followed her across the road. Bridie Fitzpatrick and I were sitting on the back Terrace wall in the Square behind the 'Dwellings'. I had been complaining at length about The Gran's weekly shopping expeditions. 'My only consolation' I told her, 'is all the years I'll get off my time in Purgatory for having to endure them'. 'Will youze for Jazzis sake get over yer self' she said crossly 'Youze won't even get a *day* off the way youze whinge about it'. 'Youze are supposed to 'Offer it up' to God and his Holy

Muddah without complaining' the miniature theologian informed me in no uncertain terms in the local vernacular. A pang of homesickness hit me as I mounted the front steps of the Hospital.

Chapter 11

The Hospital, a red brick imposing building had ten steps up to a twenty foot high front door way. The main hospital, with seventy four beds, had thirteen windows facing the road with an enclosed walkway to the right leading to the two semi-detached houses next door. 'The Wing' as we called the houses were joined internally, and contained ten private beds and housed Reverend Mother and the bedrooms, sitting and dining room of the five Registered Nurses employed by the Hospital. Access to the Wing for patients was gained via the front door of the Hospital while the Staff Nurses had direct access through their own front door. The front door of the Hospital had a generous vestibule area to wipe your feet and deposit umbrellas then another three steps were mounted to the ground floor hall. This had a grand square marble floor and splendid staircase. Clockwise was Sr. Marie's Office, Matron's Office, St Peters Ward, the corridor to the Chapel, the lift, stairs to the basement, St. Joseph's 4 bedded room, Sr. Josephine's Office, the switchboard, the corridor to the Wing, which also lead off to the Sewing Room and Laundry, then the ascending stairs and finally the Operating Theatre just to the right of the front door. Apart from the hall most of the floors were parquet, with hardwearing linoleum on some corridors.

St. Peter's Ward was a six bedded male room leading through to two four bedded rooms and a single bedded room. The four bedded St. Joseph's room had female beds. Ascending the stairs there was a further six female bed in St. Anne's room on the half landing. Collectively this was St. Peters Semi Private Ward and gave St. Peter's 15 male and 10 female beds overall. Sr. Josephine was also responsible for the ten private beds on the Wing.

The first floor has male and female sixteen bedded public wards and a variety of four bedded rooms and two bedded rooms on half landings and facing the back of the hospital. The latter twenty beds were reserved for Skin patients and were known as 'The Leper Colony' to me and my callous young colleagues. The basement contained the Hospital Kitchen which cooked meals for the hospital. Each of the three Wards also had its own good size kitchen served by a dumb waiter which transported food to be served cold. Hot food came up in the lift in heated electric trolleys from which Sister served the food onto plates. Also in the basement was a side entrance, a lift, the Out Patient Clinic, Dispensary, X-Ray and Radiotherapy Departments. On the ground floor the glass sided Chapel corridor faced the massive front door and drew the eye along a tunnel of light to a stained glass window whose refracted colours never failed to lift my spirits.

Following Donovan's example I hung my cloak in cubby hole off the ward kitchen and we entered Sr. Josephine's small office to hear the night report being given by 'The Suck'. Bernie Carroll was already there. 'The Suck' seemed very competent if a little obsequious and eager to please.

'I bet she made up half of that shoite' Tip said, signing for the handover of the 'Nursing Book' from which the Night Report had been extrapolated.

Our first duty when we came on a shift was to read the 'Nursing Book' which set out care needed by 'Bed ' and 'Help' patients and sign that we had done so. As we washed our hands Sr. Josephine gave her our work list for the day.

'Don't let her out of your sight'she said to Donovan, nodding in my direction,'

Tip' was a 1-5 off so we sorted out our breaks before we started, Donavan and I had first tea break at 9.30 and dinner at 12.30. The day went in a blur of activities. I mastered bed making, damp dusting and the bottle and bedpan rounds. The latter round started off badly because I forgot to warm the bedpan so the first patient nearly hit the ceiling from the shock of the cold enamel. I moved on to cleaning locker tops and bed tables. It was when I was moving a bed table back into position that I managed to upend a replenished jug of water over a patient's feet. Tip and Donavan had the bed stripped and made up again in an instant sending me off to the sluice room to measure sputum and clean the sputum mugs as a penance. At dinner time I managed to feed a patient without choking him but was not so successful with his neighbour whom I was helping to drink tea from a feeding cup on the afternoon tea round. After changing his pyjama top with me Donovan marched me into the ward kitchen and poured a cup of tea into a feeding cup and held it to my mouth.

'Drink' she ordered. 'Go on' she shouted as I hesitated.

The flow was faster than I anticipated and went up my nose splattering tea down my apron.

'Now hold it yourself and regulate it so that you can see how much you need to tilt it' she suggested'.

I choked again because standing behind Donovan in the doorway, mad with outrage, was Sr. Bernardino. I knew a profanity was likely to emanate from Donovan so I tried to warn her with my eyes. However we were both saved by Sr. Josephine entering with a cup and saucer in her hand, evidence that she had been having a quite cup of tea in her office. Eating patient's food was a sackable offence, and while drinking tea on the ward was totally disapproved of, most Sisters were not above persuading probationers to take their tea breaks on the ward when there was

no cover, or when the Wards were busy. But Sr. Bernardino was a black and white person and had been intent on blasting us if her Sister in Christ had not arrived. A look from Sr. Josephine clearly saying 'This is MY Ward' had her retreating, seething, without a word been spoken. This did not stop Sr. Josephine turning her wrath on us seeking an explanation for the tea stains down the front of my apron' Shaking her head in a mixture of exasperation and amusement she told me to go and change.
'Jezzis wept' Redmond, you're totally, totally, cursed' Donovan said in awe. 'Go down to the Chapel and bless yourself with Holy Water, or say an Act of Contrition or something, she advocated, 'My nerves are in shreds'. I ignored her exhortation knowing it would be a waste of time.
I was one of the damned.
5.00 p.m. and in our bedroom Donovan was reading a letter from home and I was heading for the bathroom before anybody else bagged it. Looking at Donovan the mystery of the odd marks on the walls behind the heads of everybody's beds was explained. Having taken off her shoes she had swivelled around on the bed and had her feet on the wall with her ankles resting on the headboard to ease her aching feet. It was a habit I soon emulated. Putting on a blouse and skirt I had the choice of going home for the evening or writing Gran a note telling her of my progress. The thought of taking a bus across the City then traversing the back street leading to home, and the worry of getting back by 10.00 p.m. persuaded me that a note would suffice. Remember, postal collection and delivery was a lot more frequent, and faster, in those long gone days.

The evening in the sitting room was uneventful and I satisfied everybody's curiosity about my background and antecedents. I realised I was expected to be a font of knowledge on dance halls, show bands and music venues, but I was a grave disappointment. My friends and I favoured the pictures, milk bars and neon lit ice cream parlours with juke boxes where we would sit and talk for hours. In fine weather we rode our bikes, or went on some lad's crossbar to picnic out on Dollymount Strand or in the Phoenix Park. We were an unsophisticated lot, at ease with boy's we'd grown up with, and not yet looking for romance. With little money and on the verge of rock and roll sweeping the world we were innocents abroad. But this culchie lot were mad for excitement, enthusiastic about céilidh and ballroom dancing and the opportunity of meeting off duty Gardaí marauding medical students, and civil servants with prospects, all three groups were off my radar.

The Garda Síochána na hÉireann in particular was anathema to my strata of society and I could just see the Gran and Annie Lawlor's face if I came home with one on my arm. The first thing they would probably notice was the lack of handcuffs, but I bet their initial question would have been 'What's she done Officer? A memory of a now retired Sergeant O'Sullivan from Store Street brings previous offences to mind. However the culchies knew very little about Dublin so I promised to expand their horizons. In reciprocation, Mary Cronin persuaded me to take on an American pen pal, and so Pte. Mervin L. Meyer entered my life. International pen pals were a phenomenon of the age and encouraged by schools and colleges as a means of propagating the faith in their far flung overseas Missions. The anticipation of the arrival of a pen and ink letter cannot be compared with the dozens of digital 'friends' who today correspond by illiterate texts and smart downloads.

Chapter 12

The next few days went by in a haze of confusion and an inability to retain the simplest information. I followed Donovan everywhere and progressed to giving out bowls of warm water to patients confined to bed and capable of washing themselves. I helped her bed bath the more incapacitated and began to realise that the patients were not just names on lists but individuals with different needs and problems. To date I knew their name and diagnosis and which bed they were in, but if you had stood them in an identity parade I would have been hard put to pick out a single one. I had been too terrified to make eye contact in case they wanted me to do anything, or ask me questions I couldn't answer, so I had avoided looking at their faces thereby making myself truly Donovan's shadow. St. Peter's Ward had no 'Skin' beds so I was aware that all the patients had cancer although the word was seldom said out loud nor was it proclaimed on the discrete notice board at the front of the Hospital which merely said Saint Anne's Hospital. It would be at least another three decades before you would see the word in an obituary. Patients came from all over Ireland for radium treatment following radical surgery in Regional hospitals. St. Anne's had it's own operating theatre where less complicated surgery and radium implants was carried out, this, and Out Patients Department was the domain of Sr. Bernardino. There were very few Dublin patients admitted because they could be treated on an Out Patient basis, or attend St. Luke's Skin and Cancer Hospital or the City of Dublin Skin and Cancer Hospital. The latter I think may have been funded to provide care for the Dublin catchment area or may have been just for proddies. The history of these small specialists voluntary Hospitals in Dublin has left a meagre paper trail.

All I knew was that all our patients were culchie's, would be with us for several weeks, seldom had visitors, and, and if terminally ill, might die in our care. On my first day on the ward Sr. Josephine had given me a small printed card and told Donovan to explain its use to me.

'It's just in case you find somebody dead' Donovan told me nonchalantly, adding 'don't worry it will never happen'

I thought I was going to throw up with anxiety. She expanded,

'The soul doesn't leave the body for about an hour after death, so you may be in time to intercede with God if somebody has not died in a state of grace'.

Holy shoite! What a responsibility. I stuck it in the back cover of my note pad in the hope I would never have to look at it again.

'I think you get a Plenary Indulgence if you ever have to use it' she said, implying that the reward for the trauma involved might be worth it.

In case the word 'resuscitation' crosses your mind, techniques were in their infancy then, and anyway we were more interested in our patient's immortal souls.

Also, in the 1950's the hospital didn't have sophisticated dependency status for categorizing patients they were simply 'Beds' 'Help' and 'Ambulant'. 'Beds' meant bed bound and having full nursing care which put them on the list for bed baths, back and mouth care, bottle and bedpan rounds and two hour turning and assistance with feeding if necessary. Some of these patients had serious looking tubes coming out of them draining mysterious fluids into large sealed bottles. 'Help' patients varied from the frail, to those on enforced bed rest so were varied in their needs from being given bowls to wash, helping them to the lavatory or providing a commode. Ambulatory patients provided self care and you think would be less trouble. Wrong, the women could whinge for Ireland, and the men were veritable Houdini's, disappearing without trace. However providing the latter were available for treatment, meals, and the ward round Sr. Josephine turned a blind eye knowing, that ambulant or not, most of these men were terminally ill. Our ambulatory women were in St. Anne's room on the half landing. They were quite capable of walking down the stairs to find one of us if they needed anything. However they were paying for the privilege of being in a semi private room and had been issued with buzzers, so why not use them and live up to the adage that the patients furthest away from the bell display board rings the call bell more often than the patients nearest to it. One or the other of them had Tip and Donavan up and down the stairs a dozen times a day.

As I lost my fear of accidently killing somebody or finding somebody dead I started taking my turn unaccompanied. I closed and opened windows, removed crumbs from beds, adjusted angle poise lamps, put oil on a squeaking bed table wheel, crawled under a bed to retrieve a ball of wool, unscrewed a bottle of Barley water, the list was endless. Looking back, with some maturity, I can see that these were lonely frightened women, some of them with a very poor prognosis, but in our youthful innocence they were a total pain in the arse.

'They think this is the feckin Gresham' Tip said in exasperation.

'Too true' Donovan retorted, 'But they're not paying Gresham prices and I'm not a bloody chamber maid'.

I stopped worrying about accidentally killing one of them, and considered ways of actually doing the deed as I trudged back up the stairs to answer yet another buzzer.

Chapter 13

My first day off found me on a bus from Leeson Park into Nelson Pillar on my way home. A cut down North Earl Street, a left at the Pro- Cathedral, a right into Lower Gloucester Place passing the Tin Chapel, then up the Bunkey Hill, down the steps into Bella Street where the back of the Artisans Dwellings hove into sight.

I had lived there since the death of my mother in 1947 and in nearby Upper Rutland Street before then. My change of abode had not meant changing school, but it did mean making new friends and, as now, that felt unsettling. By the time my younger siblings and I moved in with Gran and Granda the Artisan Dwellings were commonly called 'Buckingham Buildings' by local people although they were still known as the 'Artisans' Dwellings' on the 1939-40 Electoral Roll. Families were well established, with some of their children of an age to seek tenancies in their own right. The Breslin's, Grant's, Fitzpatrick's, Kelly's, O'Farrell's, McCarthy's and Mulhall's are some that come to mind. At one point a disgruntled prospective tenant suggested that the Artisans' Dwelling Company should rename the site 'Grants Mansions' and be done with it. There may have been some judicious rising of eyebrows, and muttered accusations of favouritism and undue influence about allocations, but the denizens, on the whole, lived in harmony. It was very much a matriarchal enclave where the women took it in turns to clean their landings and wash down their flight of stairs. They bickered about who had stolen Annie Lawlor's Jeyes Fluid, who had spilled turf debris all over the stairs, and sin of sins, who had left the landing door unbolted over night. The latter was a service to courting couples wanting a little bit of romance and privacy on their way to their respective beds.

The mother's castigated and cursed each other's children and minded them when necessary. They criticized one another, supported one another, delivered babies when a 'Bona Fide' midwife wasn't available or couldn't be afforded and laid out and waked the dead. They loaned what finery they had for christenings and weddings, and being mindful that they were a bit more fortunate than their neighbours in the tenements on the other side of the street, tried to fulfil as many of the corporal works of mercy as they could. The Georgian tenements facing the Dwellings were some of the worst in Dublin with gaping hall doors and a family to every room. They housed decent families doing their best in dire circumstances but lacked the security of the Artisans' tenancies and the co-operative way of living engendered by its structure. Dublin humour was part of everyday life and nicknames were common. Insults were exchanged on a regular basis. Being called a 'gunner eyed git', 'scabby little shite', an 'impetent' brat, or a 'bockety arsed bowsie' were said without malice, while some commands from our elders were confusing, or physically impossible, such as 'shut your gob and ate yer dinner', or 'if youz break yer neck, don't come runnin ta me', and 'do youz wannit now, or will youz wait 'til yez get it'? An exasperated neighbour said to me one day 'Hold on, I'll see if she's up me hole pickin daisy's' when I asked where her daughter was. Gran thought that was very 'common' and said 'what would you expect from yer wan when 'she's worn a groove across the road' e.g. 'spent her life in the pawnshop'.

As I walked along Bella Street, which still had some of its old cobbles, but was now a patchwork quilt of asphalt as a memento of work done by the utility companies, I noticed for the first time how shabby the neighbourhood looked. Although the smell of cabbage cooking and the waft of pigs from nearby Summerhill Place were familiar I was newly aware of them after the quiet refinement of Northbrook Road. It dawned on me that out in the suburbs I hadn't heard a seagull or church bell since leaving home. Gran had the table set for dinner when I reached No. 31 and a pot of tea newly brewed. Annie was sitting by the range waiting patiently to hear all the news. Our fare was going to be stuffed sheep's heart and colcannon. I hid a smile because whatever the shortcomings of the Nurses Home eating offal was not one of them. Throughout my childhood with Gran, apart from the occasional broiled chicken, coddle or silverside, our daily protein was offal of every type and description. This included sheep's head's, tripe, heart's, liver, ox tail, and calves feet, all scourged out of poor Mr Butler one of the butchers on Summerhill. He would point to the prices painted in white paste on his shop window in vain. Mr. Quinn, our pork butcher, was made of sterner stuff. However even he succumbed to the Gran's bartering, or more accurately, battering. She claimed kinship to him via her mother. From him she bought black and white pudding, crubeens, and pig's cheeks which she used to roast. Having fleeced him on the offal she would then threaten to go along to his competitors Granby's, Hefner's or Stein's for her sausages telling him his were more expensive. It was pointless arguing with her that his were a better product so he'd throw in a couple of extra sausages to keep her quiet. The only thing we all refused to eat was kidneys. Our corny joke about offal was *It's awful but we like it*. And I did. I saw them both looking at me in stunned revulsion as I bolted my food, and I could read their minds as they thought '*Oh my God, who is this pig?*' A week was all it had taken.

The day flew by with neighbours coming and going with dozens of questions and wanting to see me in uniform. I hadn't thought to dress the part but made promises for my next day off. The day flew. I was afloat with tea and questions and before I knew it I was on my way into O'Connell Street to meet Bridie Fitz from work. Gran saw me on my way with a big bag of potato cakes she'd griddled, and a quarter of butter in waxed paper. Sharing a Banana split Bridie and I spent an hour catching up. We promised to meet up again on my next day off but I realised that with the complexity of my off duty rota I would have to write and let her know. With no one having landlines phoning was out. The only phone in the Nurses Home was next door in the Nuns front hall and was only to be used by us in dire emergencies. I have no recollection of it ever being used. Back at the Home before eight I was toasting Grans potato cakes on the sitting room fire while one of the others put butter on with the aid of a ruler.

'Runo it mightbe worthhavinto putupwid a Jackeen after all' Bina Corcoran said sucking the butter off her fingers.

Chapter 14

Mikeen McCafferty was dying. He lay in a bed in the six bedded room with the curtains pulled. He was emaciated and jaundiced having fought a losing battle with pancreatic cancer. A bachelor in his early forties he had a sister and mother in far off Tourmakeady who were trying to keep the little subsistence farm going. The rest of the family were scattered to the winds of emigration so were unlikely to return for sad good-byes. His sister had visited a few days previously begging him to come home for what little time he had left. 'Ah, musha I might as well stay here in comfort' he had told her. I didn't know whether that was a compliment to our care, or said more about his home circumstances including the worry of creeping debt, probably a mixture of both. He was still fully conscious and had been joking with the other patients prior to the curtains been drawn.

'Don't forget to tell dem all, Mikeen' one of the others who had shaved him earlier joked.

'Sure they're only venials' Mikeen retorted weakly.

Tip and I were putting a clean counterpane on the bed while Sr. Josephine was creating an alter on the locker top. A small lace cloth, two candles in holders, a standing crucifix and an asperonium of Holy water were all set out leaving room in the centre for the small box containing holy oil and the consecrated wafer the priest would bring. Mikeen McCafferty was about to receive Extreme Unction and Viaticum. Frightening names for the three sacraments involved; Confession, the Last Rites and Communion, nowadays innocuously called Anointing the Sick. When the priest arrived the men moved away to give space for privacy, Sr. Josephine lit the candles and draping a hand towel over my arm told me to hover out of earshot and when the priest came out from behind the curtains to escort him across the Ward to the hand basin to allow him to wash his hands. A task so simple, you could entrust it to a child of five. Ya think? Hearing Sr. Bernardino's voice in the corridor I glided out of sight to the right of Mikeen's screened bed thereby missing the Priest as he exited left. Assuming he was still behind the curtains I waited, then with her usual stealth, Sr. Bernardino was upon me, and with the swiftness of the *Shee an Gannon* wrenched the towel from my arm.

'You useless moronic amadan' she hissed at me taking the towel into the ward kitchen where the Priest having washed his hands was drying them on a damp tea towel.

I was numb with mortification. Tip pushing me back behind Mikeen's curtains whispering 'Find Sr. Josephine and tell her' 'Don't give C.J. the satisfaction of being the one to do it'. Sage advice. I'm sure Sr. Josephine could cheerfully have rung my neck but she found a more fitting means of showing her displeasure by making me clean all the bed wheels.

Mikeen Mc McCafferty lived for several more days, initially with his curtains pulled back so that he could participate in ward life, but as the comfort of morphine eased his way from a quiet inward looking decline into peaceful unconsciousness his side curtains were drawn to give him privacy. Eventually his breathing became shallow then erratic and laboured, and as he drifted away the other patients were told the Prayers for the Dying would be said giving them the opportunity to stay and participate or leave the ward. They opted to stay as Sr. Josephine lit a candle, and winding his rosary beads around his hands she intoned '*Prodeo o Sarcalogos animus ex is universitas* and continued the prayer commending his soul to God. She then led the men and us in decade of a rosary.

When his Cheyne Stokes breathing ceased everybody held back tears. His body being 'the Temple of the Holy Spirit' we waited the obligatory hour for his soul to depart, and then she and Donovan washed and laid him out. The moment of transition from his fading life into a peaceful death had a profound effect on me in that I lost any fear of death I might have harboured. The men gathered at the ward table to play cards enjoying the extra round of tea Sr. Josephine had sanctioned. Apart from Hospices that began to be established in the 60's this inclusive way of dealing with death has long gone, now it is cold and clinical, monitored by machine, hidden away in side rooms and Godless.

Chapter 15

As the end of my first month hove into sight I had quite a few ticks in the Observation column in my 'Schedule of Nursing', and Donovan and Tip had been generous in filling in my Participation activities. I was now about to spend the morning working with Sr. Josephine to see if I had progressed enough to be deemed to have developed any Proficiencies in basic nursing care. I handed her the Schedule as she put on her white nursing apron.
'All right Nurse I am your helper for the morning so explain your routine to me' she said with a smile and indicated with her hand that I was to precede her onto the ward.

The blood supply to my brain seemed to cut off as I entered the six bedded male ward. The men had been warned in advance by Tip to be on their best behaviour but they could have been swinging from the curtain rails for all the notice I took. The routine that I could perform like a robot was lost somewhere in my unconscious brain. Out of the corner of my eye I saw Donovan mouthing at me and indicating a breakfast tray. The automatic pilot light went on. Collect breakfast trays – fill sterilizer - bedpan and bottle round – bowl round – make beds – damp dust window sills etc. - clean locker tops and bed tables – wash sputum mugs - replenish water jugs – fill in intake and output charts – clear and clean Tip and Donovan's dressing trolleys - wash instruments – put instruments and syringes on to sterilise - tidy sluice room and answer buzzers. Tip obviously hadn't told the women on the half landing I was being assessed so they buzzed as normal. However what was not normal was that neither she, nor Donovan answered any of the buzzers, watching in amusement as Sr. Josephine and I trudged up and down the

stairs. The morning seemed endless but apart from me losing all sense of co-ordination was progressing without disaster. Bed making had become an effortless task for me. My fellow bed makers and I worked in total synchronicity producing perfectly mitred corners, taut draw sheets, counterpanes centred with an equidistant fall on either side, pillows plumped up and openings facing away from the door, and last, but not least, the bed wheels kicked straight. This morning bed making was a nightmare. I was far too fast for Sr. Josephine. When she was at the top of the bed I was at the foot. She tried to be quicker as I tried to slow down which seemed to make it worse. However she saw the funny side of it saying
'Well Nurse, how do you think I'm doing'?

Coming up to lunch I checked the Nursing Book and realised that for once I wasn't rushing to 'get done' as I normally was. We went back to her office for her to write up the report and I was feeling confident I had done quite well. I could see 'Proficiencies' being signed off one after the other until it came to 'Time Management' where she wrote 'For Review'. I was stunned and looked at her in surprise.

'Tell me Nurse, what did you forget' she asked twirling her pen in her fingers?

I racked my brains. Perhaps she had noticed I had nearly let the sterilizer boil dry, or had forgotten the promised cup of tea for a patient who had missed the tea round.

'Take a look at us Nurse and tell me what you see' she said.

Apart from both of us being a bit pink from the morning's exertions I saw nothing. Then the penny dropped I still had yesterdays apron on. I had given no thought to our tea break.

'You worked me like a slave all morning and never gave me a break' she said.

'If I had been a new Probationer in your care I would have every reason to complain about your lack of consideration for my well being'.

I was stunned. How could I be so stupid?

'We'll review your time management next time she said handing back my 'Schedule'.

Tip and Donovan fell about the sluice room laughing when they heard I had worked Sr. Josephine through her morning break.

'Why didn't you remind me' I wailed? Having gone on separate breaks they hadn't noticed.

'Anyway, nobody but a total feckin eejit would forget about a tea break' Tip responded scathingly.

~ FEBRUARY ~
Chapter 16

Sr. Marie was a little china doll of a nun. She had dark eyebrows, bright blue eyes, rosy cheeks and lips that looked pink enough to have been touched up by lipstick. However she was as God made her. At 5'2" without her soaring head gear she was small and neat and young and we all liked her. She was the hospital Lady Almoner and Bursar, and more importantly our Pay Master. On the last Wednesday of the month we went to her office to receive, and sign for, our remuneration. £3p 2s 6p doesn't sound a lot for working more than 50 hours a week. In comparison I had been paid £1p 5s a day for working in O'Leary's emporium in Fairview on Saturdays. However, at that time St. Anne's was one of the few hospitals to offer training *and* pay, and I knew that when I applied to any Hospital to do my General Training I would have to pay £200 for the privilege, or emigrate to the United Kingdom to train *and* get a salary. I said this to Donovan who looked at me in a mock pitying way her training fees assured for further training by her farmer daddy.

'Jezzis Redmond, you're a scream, have you been reading 'Pollyanna' she inquired sardonically?

No, I was just being realistic. Coming from Summerhill I knew I was part of a generation whose future would be on a foreign shore. An impoverished country, a dismal economic environment and De Valera's deeply conservative Ireland would not be able to meet either our aspirations or expectations in the furtherance of a career. Our exodus was rationalized by many as a temporary expedient until things improved at home, but within five years my address book contained addresses of fellow ex-pats in Canada, Australia, New Zealand and the USA. To this day they have remained part of the Irish Diaspora and are still talking about 'going home'. Those of us who couldn't afford a transatlantic flight, or weren't eligible for the various cheap emigration tickets available to families, headed for the North Wall or Dun Laoighire to take the boat to England.

That evening the sitting room was buzzing with talk and plans to spend our hard earned cash as soon as possible. Those of a practical nature considered new stockings as a priority, while the flighty decided that a few more darns would see them through. Admission fees for dances came high on everybody's list apart from mine. The acquisition of a new frock was a must for Phil Kelly but would clean her out for the month.

'There's always the Hill' I said echoing Lena Breslin from the Dwellings.

None of them had ever heard of Cumberland Street second hand market so I told Kelly I would take her to have a look around. There was some disquiet from Pat Harbourne about wearing other people's clothes which I thought was rich coming from somebody who thought nothing of borrowing finery for a dance. A fry up at 'The Singing Kettle' in Leeson Street and a Tea at Bewley's in Grafton Street was on everybody's list.

Later in the week Phil, the Mc Carthy sisters and I set out for 'the Hill' on our morning off. We heard the Market before we saw it, sellers, encouraging buyers to examine their goods, and buyers, pretending to be outraged by the prices being asked. The culchies were wide eyed with wonder descending on racks of dresses, coats, handbags and shoes, ignoring toys, gramophone records, pictures, old prams and ephemera. Phil had fallen in love with a shiny emerald green frock and was being measured up by the seller, a dealer, intent on making a sale.

'I can do it for yiz for two quid' she said to the innocent culshie who was just about to open her mouth and her purse to accept with delight.

'Are youze feckin jokin or wah' I said in my best Summerhill vernacular.

The dealer looked at me in surprise and I saw the glint of determination in her eye at the prospect of a haggling match. The Grans training kicked in as I denigrated the quality of the material in Dublineze, pointing out that it was dry clean only as I sniffed the detachable cotton underarm pads, and shook my head in disappointment at the seam finishing.

'We'll give youze five bob for it' I said with finality.

'Seven and six' she hissed venomously not wanting to be beaten down.

Much to Phil's delight we got it for six shillings. Gran would have been well pleased but I knew that Sr. Monica my old elocution teacher would be appalled. The good woman had spent years figuratively knocking Summerhill Dublineze out of me. Her mantra was 'You may be growing up in Summerhill, but by the time you leave North William Street School you will speak as if you live in Foxrock'. Well she was right, good diction had helped me get in to St. Anne's, because I did sound as if I came from a leafier suburb, but I was born and bred in Summerhill and the Dublin street vernacular was my mother tongue. I could insult and streel as good as any dealer.

Puss and Mary were much more interested in shoes. Sparkly, high heeled and totally impractical were purchased despite my concerns, but for a pittance. I had been going through the old seventy eights, something I used to do with my grandfather and I spent sixpence on a John Mc Cormack record for the Gran. I realised that time had flown and that we were going to be hard put to make it back to the Nurses Home in time for dinner before going on a late duty at 1.00. We set off at a run using short cuts that only a north Dubliner would know, turning into O' Connell Street just as a bus for Ballsbridge came along. We made it back in time to throw on our uniforms, and with ten minutes to devour our congealing dinners we set an all time record. I remembered later that I had forgotten to tell Kelly to leave the frock out to air. Cumberland Street Market was not called a flea market for nothing.

This was the first of several sojourns to the market. Once the culchie's got the hang of bargaining, using as a rule of thumb, that whatever the price quoted, the item would be worth only a quarter of what was asked, I left them to it. The emerald green dress, which turned out to be top quality silk, graced many a dance hall, on several bodies, until it left for Galway when Phil completed her training. Every month Sr. Marie used to try to persuade us to start a savings account. 'If you saved five shillings a month it would be a little something to fall back on' she's say, but being young and invincible we took no notice and were scraping around for pennies days before pay day.

Chapter 17

Back on duty Donovan told me Matron wanted to see me. All my sins passed before my eyes, the three most recent being the broken medicine glass I had buried in the dirty dressings bag, the sheet gone off to the laundry stained by a galley pot full of gentian violet I has spilt on it, and the Cheadle forceps I had dropped down the bed pan washer, which had still to be retrieved. Or, perhaps she had already heard about the Market; a guilty conscience feeds a fertile imagination.

'I think she only wants you to sign on' Donovan said in an effort to reassure me.

'Sign on what' I asked my mouth dry. Sign on for the Noviciate? Sign on for servitude for life? Donate my body to Science? The possibilities seemed endless.

'For the first month you can walk out of here with a days notice on either side, but from now on one or the other of you will have to give a months' notice, that is unless you are accused of *gross professional misconduct*' she said smirking.

God, what did *that* entail?

'Do something about your cap before you go in' she advised 'and don't forget your Schedule'.

Sr. Mary Joseph, aka Matron, aka Reverend Mother bade me enter, ignored me for an eternity then scrutinised me from head to toe before indicating I had permission to be seated. Not a word had been exchanged yet so I had the urge to open my mouth and babble. A memory of Hermione Rowe a ferocious teacher in my past flashed before me so I remained silent placing my Schedule on the desk within reach. Hermione's silences had been a form of skilled intimidation and oneupmanship, and in the year I had been with her I had survived what felt like a baptism of fire so I considered that I had become a proficient antagonist. With Hermione the first one to speak was deemed the loser, so I now waited in silent expectation for the Rev to begin.

I sat on the chair, back straight, hands relaxed, feet square on the floor and a look of attentive anticipation on my face. I tried hard not to react as she cracked first.

'Well, Nurse Redmond, you seem to have made good progress since you joined us, do you intend to stay' she said looking at me over her glasses.

'Yes, Matron I said, firmly, realising I was fully committed to see the year through.

She explained the implications in detail but the only one I absorbed was that I was to have an allocated three hours study time a week. I knew from fellow Probationers that the three hours often fell in their off duty time. Because of our staggered starting dates most learning was self directed, but when it involved visits to the College of Surgeons or Mercer Street Hospital who both allowed us access to lectures which were relevant to our specialist training, our off duty time for the day was eaten up. I signed the contract without reading it and I would swear there was a look of disappointment on her face that I had not made her wait while I had done so.

I was anticipating her permission to rise when she said

'Before you go Nurse there's just one more thing' and passed me a piece of paper. 'You will need to purchase this list of books'.

I couldn't have been more shocked if she had lobbed a hand grenade into my lap. Being used to borrowing books from Libraries I had assumed that there would be a stock of books available to me. The list was a blur but the total cost glowed in neon; £12. 10s.

Jezzis wept! That was four months' salary eaten up.

I can't have hidden the look of shock on my face because she continued condescendingly;

'Of course you can get them second hand'.

'Knowing your family circumstances I'm sure Sr. Marie could find a little bursary' she said with gracious benevolence, heaping fire on her insult.

Pride and rage took over in equal measure. 'Thank you Matron' I said through gritted teeth.

'There will be no problem', and grabbing my Schedule left the room without being dismissed.

Donovan found me bawling and banging bedpans in the sluice room and assumed I had been kicked out. When I told her about the bursary she called me all the eejits under Gods heaven, and I could hear the families in the Dwellings echoing her sentiments, but with more explicit profanities. However I knew Gran would understand. She had an anathema of Charities having had to resort to them when Granda was out of work because of his Larkinite sympathies during the 1913 'Lock Out'. It was one thing to accept a bit of help from the nuns in North William Street who knew the family from the time my Aunt's had been at school there, but to have this lot making assumptions about us because I came from Summerhill was an entirely different kettle of fish, and smacked of the scrimped and iced variety of charity. Our relationship with North William Street was not a one way street. Sheila was generous in support of the Convent and Gran participated in their 'Invite an Orphan to tea' campaign, which is precisely the same kind of patronage I was objecting to, but was hugely enjoyed by the children involved. To them, the tea was incidental; it was the opportunity and freedom to run wild playing out in the local streets they enjoyed most.

My next half day I set off for the big second-hand bookshop along Ormond Quay with £5 in my purse. Gran and Annie Lawlor always pressed a few coins in my hand when I visited so my current wealth amounted to a little over £6 but I had left enough at the Nurses Home for sanitary towels, and a new pair of stockings if the need arose. The bookshop was a labyrinth of rooms with towering bookshelves of esoteric and arcane volumes on every subject under the sun. I eventually found the Medical – Nursing section and was able to tell the culchies on my return that this was the place to meet medical students without having to fork out the price of a ticket to a Dance Hall. Having found what I wanted I realised that the total price came to nearly £6. The elderly tired looking woman with birds nest hair who was restacking the shelves saw me dithering around trying to decide which books to take and leave. Eventually she came over and I explained my dilemma.

'Where are you training' she asked.

When she heard it was St. Anne's Skin and Cancer Hospital she shuddered and said

'I don't know how you young girls do it'.

Taking the books from me she ushered me over to a quiet corner, and rummaging in her cardigan pocket produced a rubber and quickly erased the pencilled prices on the fly leafs, reducing the overall cost to £4. 5s I was speechless with gratitude.

'Now, not a word' she said conspiratorially 'take them over to that dozy young git on the till, he wouldn't know the price of second-hand book if his job depended on it'. 'Unfortunately it doesn't' she continued caustically, tapping her pencil on the side of her nose, 'Nepotism' she murmured.

'Ah' I said nodding in sympathy.

How right she was, giving a cursory glance to the books he wrapped them in brown paper, secured the package with string and took my money with an automatic

'Come again, Miss and I was out the door, relieved and exhilarated.

Back on the Ward I informed Sr. Josephine that I had all the books needed to start training. She looked pleased and telling me that there would be no formal lectures until some more Probationers started set me some reading to do from 'Practical Nursing', 'Clinical Bacteriology' and 'Anatomy and Physiology', three of my textbooks. This was to add theory to the practical skills I was to acquire before next month's review. Wednesdays mornings were designated as my study time but I knew from others that getting three hours break as well as three hours for study was pie in the sky. And so it proved. The talk of new Probationers had reminded me that Donovan and the Mc Carthy sisters only had a month left to do. However the good news was that I would be allocated to St. Peter's Ward for another two months.

Chapter 18

In my capacity as an appendage to Donovan's apron strings I had participated in a lot of care without having responsibility for the outcome. Now I would be expected to become proficient in some aspects of that care. God bless the tolerance of the patients as I took, and, re-took their blood pressure and temperatures. I'm sure the sleeping Paddy Joe Delaney had forgiven me long before he died for pulling the curtains round his bed when I found him pulseless. Shouting at an ambulant patient to find Sister, I commenced the Prayer of Commendation to God, from Sr. Josephine's little card. I didn't get much further than 'Go forth O Christian soul from this world' when the poor man opened his eyes and looked at me with a mixture of terror and confusion. The ambulant patient grabbed the first passing nun he could find, unfortunately, it was Sr. Bernardino.

Donovan was right, I was cursed. She was so incandescent with rage that I shut off her rant by concentrating on a pulsating vein by her left eye and tried to calculate what her pulse rate was. Heeding Tips' previous advice I went to get Sr. Josephine's ear first. She said nothing walking off at a surprisingly brisk pace until she reached Paddy Joe's bed where Sr. B. was plumping up his pillows, and making herself generally officious. She was about to launch into another diatribe when Sr. Josephine said icily

'A moment of your time Sister and ushered her from the room.

 I knew by now that Sr. Bernardino's interference in her ward was a thorn in Sr. Josephine's side, and her anger was probably the only sin she had to declare at Saturday afternoon Confessions. The priest alone knows what C.J. confessed, and I was beyond redemption. As soon as the nuns left the ward general hilarity broke out.

'Holy Moly, Nurse, you didn't half scare the bejezzis out of me' Paddy Joe said 'I thought I was a gonner, and me supposed to be going home tomorrow'.

The humiliation I was feeling was passing and I was now sufficiently at ease with the patients to accept the craic and to give as good as I got, offering to finish what I had started in case he died in the night. Tip came along to help out with the TPR's. It was a ten minute job for an experienced nurse. I had already taken forty five thereby delaying the tea trolley, not to mention forfeiting my own morning break. The TPR tray was set with a galley pot full of cotton wool balls and six thermometers in a glass meat paste jar filled with surgical spirit. This allowed for up to six temperatures to be taken at the same time while pulses and respirations could be taken for a quarter of a minute and multiplied by four. I had reached nowhere near this standard of efficiency, and had actually broken a thermometer a day since I started, leaving us with three. I had to write this in the Broken Thermometer Book and was supposed to take the shards to Sr. Josephine for replacement. In theory 10d for each thermometer would be deducted from my salary, but it never was. Despite Tips complaints I didn't think this was an opportune time to confess the breakages, so dashed off to get a clean apron before I got into more trouble. I saw nothing of Sr. Josephine until just before I went off duty. In fact I sought her out, not wanting to spend the night worrying about what was in store. I went to the Ward Office to find the door closed and hearty laughter from inside. I put my ear to the door and realised that Mr. Delaney's demise was the topic of the amusement. I knocked and was ushered in by Sr. Vincent from St. Vincent's Ward, the male public ward upstairs.

She left, smiling broadly, which gave me hope as I faced Sr. Josephine.

'Tell me what happened Nurse' she asked?

I explained as best I could. She said nothing for what seemed like an age and I was tempted once again to babble.

'Well Nurse' she said leaning back in her chair. 'I can't fault your ability to deal with a crisis, but did you not think to look for any signs of respiration before pronouncing him dead' she asked caustically?

She went on to explain that some patient's pulses were very difficult to detect, so it was good practice to count the respirations first.

'I think a review of your observation skills should be part of your next report' she said standing up and showing me the door.

'I've apologised to Mr. Delaney' I said obsequiously, hoping to gain her approval.

'Yerra I wouldn't worry too much about Paddy Joe Delaney' she retorted tartly, 'Thinking he was about to meet his Maker sooner than he anticipated will do him no harm at all', it might even concentrate his mind on his immortal soul, rather than the winner of the 3.30.

Chapter 19

Staff Nurse Connie Duffy was a desiccated sinewy woman with permed grey hair and horn-rimmed glasses. She had been an Army Nurse in England and having been discharged at fifty five was supplementing her army gratuity by working on to retirement pension age at St. Anne's. Although she looked as if she suffered from chronic indigestion she was quite pleasant and fiercely efficient. She mostly worked in Theatre and Out Patients, but when a Ward or the Wing was particularly busy she was sent to help out. Sr. Josephine decided that she should observe my two allocated bed baths. Most baths to date had always been with either Tip or Donovan doing the washing and me setting up the trolley, getting the patient' ready and helping with the drying. On this on occasion I was doing the washing. The procedure had firm modesty rules which made the situation embarrassing for all concerned. It put me in mind of the dance of the seven veils where flashes of skin where fleetingly exposed. Instead of veils we had towels. The most important being the towel that covered the patient from neck to pubes. For some reason this towel was called 'the blanket'. The procedure for male patients was to remove the pyjama top and cover them with 'the blanket', wash their face ears and neck and upper limbs with a white face flannel. The patient was rolled to have his back washed and then rolled back to have his front done. For the latter the modesty blanket covered his chest and the Nurse, putting her hand under the blanket washed as far as his umbilicus. The pyjama top was put on and the blanket was moved down to cover the pubic area; the pyjama bottoms were removed and the patient was given a blue face flannel, for hygiene purposes, and expected to wash and dry his genitalia while the Nurse practiced *Custody of the Eyes* and made light conversation. This was difficult for some very ill patients but nobody had told me what to do in such circumstances. I had observed both my mentors ignoring any problem in this area. Legs and feet were then washed, the patient redressed, hair combed, mouth care carried out, bed made and the patient left looking neat and tidy.

Duffy checked my trolley before we ventured into the Ward. She nodded in approval, disappeared momentarily, returning with several sheets of Izal lavatory paper which she placed on the bottom shelf. Our first patient was Ger Reilly. Ger, who was weakened by several bouts of radium treatment for Hodgkin's disease, a cancer of the lymphatic system was a sixty year old bachelor who lived with a half brother out on the Beara Peninsula in Kerry. I explained what we were going to do and he raised a weary arm half in acknowledgement but more in resignation. I started off ineffectively dabbing his face trying not to be too rough. Duffy sucked her teeth and glared a me in exasperation, and before I could dab Ger to death, swopped sides with me with a firm 'Let me do this one'. A startled Ger got the scrubbing of a lifetime. No modesty blanket here. His rib indented torso shone with cleanliness, and his knobbly spine and protruding scapulas got an invigouring mentholated spirit rub topped off with baby powder. Duffy granted him some modesty by momentarily covering his genitalia while we removed his pyjama bottoms. She soaped the blue face flannel, twitched the blanket back out of her way, and reaching for a sheet of lavatory paper she laid a piece on Ger's penis and lifting up the organ, and holding it between two fingers, gave his scrotum and inguinal creases a thorough wash and rinse. All this was done while she kept up a conversation on the price spring lambs were fetching. I didn't know where to look but it seemed less embarrassing to look at Ger's genitalia than his face. 'Dry' she said passing me a piece of loo paper. And holding the penis as she had, dry I did, observing some inflammation in the inguinal creases from previous hit and miss washing. I realised then that Duffy was a good nurse, and when she told me to apply some antiseptic cream I did so with no embarrassment. When we finished with Ger Reilly he looked like a well scrubbed hair slicked urchin and was sitting up in bed looking forward to his dinner.

Our next patient was a weepy depressed female with a newly formed colostomy. She winced and cringed every time I touched her and I expected Duffy to take over again. However she just sat on the bed and took the woman's hand saying 'You probably had a bath yesterday before your op, so how about we just help you do your bits and doll you up'. Bits? Dolling up? Not part of Sr. Josephine's vocabulary but I was willing to learn. Bits turned out to be armpits and genital area or 'the wet bits' as Duffy called them. I tried to keep a straight face and was now prepared to be quite pragmatic about genital areas. I was about to zone in and apply the face flannel when the affronted patient took the flannel and attempted to do it herself. I resisted the temptation to say 'you'll never get the soap out of the cracks'. Again Duffy showed what a good nurse she was. She went off to the sluice room returning with a bedpan and a jug of warm water invited the patient to sit on the bed pan while she poured the water over the her genital area. 'Dolling up' was accomplished by putting on deodorant, a clean nightdress, styling her hair and leaving her applying her make up in preparation for visitors. Another satisfied customer and two unorthodox bed baths completed. I had learned more about good patient care in a morning than I had in the previous month. As well as for bed baths, and shaving the area before surgery, I went on to use Duffy's toilet paper technique when placing a urinal in position for men who were too incapacitated to do so themselves. This prevented a wet drawsheet as a result of the 'hope for the best' method used by nurses too embarrassed to check that the patient's penis was inside the bottle. It was a subject that was not covered in my Practical Nursing textbook but during my nursing career I never forgot Duffy and her Izal, which in time became Kleenex.

Chapter 20

The Suck came off night duty and was allocated to Theatre and Outpatients. Ordinarily a month working 8 to 5 with one day a week relieving on the Wards would be regarded as a cushy number but being under the supervision of Sr. Bernardino for anybody but The Suck this would have been purgatory. Mary Cronin joined Sheila Brady on nights saving Sheila's sanity and immortal soul, Sheila admitting that she was having overwhelming urges to kill The Suck. Up to this point I had had very little contact with her but now that she back on days she set out to cultivate me. I found her pleasant enough but her intrusive questioning about my background and her fishing for an invitation to Grans annoyed me. She took to joining us in the sitting room in the evening eager to be part of the conversation, and while most of the group were polite to her, nobody ever went out with her, or included her if they were going dancing. I felt very sorry for her, but a feeling of intense irritation usually over rode any urge I had to befriend her. I hated being on duty with her because of the covetous eyes she cast on any biscuits or chocolate the patients visitors brought in. We were all aware that most patients' visitors travelled the length or breath of the country to visit; fares were expensive so visits were few and far between. We therefore stored what few goodies the patient's received in their bedside lockers, politely refusing offers to take a bar of chocolate or a packet of biscuits. The ambulant patients were different in that they could go out to the local shop, or get one of us to do a bit of shopping in our off duty time, so we didn't feel bad about accepting a little reward from them. However 'The Suck' was shameless and unlike everybody else never brought anything to the sitting room to share out. Commensurate with her return to days I noticed that a half a crown was missing from my purse as well as a half packet of biscuits, both had been in my locked wardrobe. I mentioned it in the sitting room to discover that several others, including The Suck, had also had small amounts stolen. The Suck insinuated that it was probably Mary, the maid resulting in Donovan furiously tearing strips off her. Although the thefts were small, they created an uneasy atmosphere in the house, but nobody was prepared to go to Sr. Agnes about it. When I came off duty one evening and found my wardrobe unlocked I'd had enough and took myself off home to borrow a piece of equipment that I thought might solve the problem. It took several days, but when I came across The Suck with a bandaged hand being sent home for a couple days, I knew our problem was resolved. 'Caught her fingers in a door' was the official version. A well placed mouse trap has the same result. I immediately felt guilty about trapping her fingers, but this was mitigated by the fact that she had tried to implicate Mary. For a maid to be accused of theft would put an end to her employment prospects and the roof over her head. When the Suck didn't return from sick leave everybody heaved a sigh of relief.

I'd like to say I soon forgot her, but I didn't. She must have been a very unhappy girl to have alienated so many people, but none of us cared enough to find out anything about her, or wonder why she was so needy. It is indicative of our callousness that a few months down the line none of us could remember her name. That was remedied in the most unexpected way by Maggie, Donovan's contact in the sewing room. Having forgotten to put my personal laundry out for collection I took it surreptitiously across to the laundry to add it to the pile. To do this I had to pass

Maggie's domain so I had brought a 3d bar of Cadbury's to sweeten her ire. Maggie, reminded me of a younger version of the Gran. A skinny whippet of a woman in a blue serge dress, in her forties, she had a clean carbolic smell, dark hair scraped back in a bun. She seldom smiled and was given to 'moods' but today she was not only amenable, but keen for somebody to chat to so I broached the subject of The Suck's name, not of course calling her 'The Suck', but the Probationer from Meath.

'Ah 'the Suck' you mean. She said, looking at me with her shrewd dark eyes and told me the name which I of course instantly remembered. I told her I was sorry I had not been nicer to her.

'She was a poor wee cratereen sure enough' she acknowledged 'but a weasel to the core and light fingered with it. 'I had to be careful to watch her going through the 'Reclaim shelf' she said, nodding at the shelf where unidentified personal laundry was laid out.

'I'd feel sorry for her just the same' she said, concentrating on re-threading a sewing machine.

'Her parents died young, and she was taken in by two maiden Aunts. Her two brothers were put in an orphanage, but the Aunts took her on sufferance, probably more concerned with what the neighbour's would say than with her welfare' she talked as she slowly started treadling the machine. 'They put her boarding as soon as the nuns would take her. I'd say the poor kid learned her 'sucking' ways early in life both at school and at home' she said as she finished the run of sewing, and looking at me with a sad smile said 'now that's between you and me and these four walls.

I looked at her with new eyes. I knew nothing about her background but suspected a certain amount had been in institutional care. She wore no wedding ring to indicate her marital status but that meant nothing. In the Summerhill

Pawnshop wedding rings were in and out like a cuckoo in a clock, and often lay unredeemed if the basic necessities overwhelmed the need for adornment.

Chapter 21

Well into my second month I realized I had no idea what was going on in the world. Apart from catching the odd headline in a patient's newspaper I might as well be living on the dark side of the moon. Coming from a home where the murmur of a radio was constantly in the background and news available from a paper boy on every street corner I felt a sense of deprivation and mental apathy. With no time for the luxury of mooching down to the local Library for recreational reading I was left with time to engage with the work I was set in my text books. While I may have had the time, I had neither the energy nor the inclination. There was not a single reading lamp in the whole house, which cut reading to a day time activity, so it was usually done during the day in off duty time. It was also done under the bedclothes to keep warm. This was a fatal combination. I only had to start on a Chapter in my Bacteriology assignment before my eyes began to droop. Would I ever get to know how many gram positive spore forming types of bacilli's there were? Did I *really* need to know about bubonic plague and cholera?

What I *did* know was that Sr. Josephine was not going to let me loose with the dressing's trolley until I understood the modes and types of infections and the aseptic techniques necessary to prevent them. Antibiotics, still in their infancy were a bit of a hit and miss affair for treating infections so prevention was paramount. At a time when nothing was disposable there were sterilizers and an autoclave, in every sluice room, and for cleaning we had several corrosive compounds that resulted in red, dry, chapped hands, hands that identified you as a nurse. Hail rain or snow every window in the Hospital was thrown open to kill germs during bed making, so to have a patient get an infected wound was a total disgrace, and the poor patient was interrogated by Sister as to who had as much as looked at the wound. For every dressing we did we had to 'gown up' and wear a mask and gloves. To intimate that the patient may have been infected during surgery was enough to send Sr. Bernardino into paroxysms of rage, so it was usually laid at the door of the Ward Sister, and no Ward Sister was ever going to let the buck stop there, or allow blame be put on her staff. The patient was never deemed to be at fault although their debilitated state often left them prone to infection. As far as Sister was concerned the probable culprit would have been one of the doctors, and she was always looking for evidence to prove her theory. Then one day I had the evidence to hand to her on a plate when I observed a doctor 'taking a peep' at a post op colostomy which was a 'dirty' operation and then going to examine mastectomy, a 'clean' operation without washing his hands. I was appalled.

'What did you say to him' asked a disgusted Tip.

'Nothing' I saw wilting under her tone 'He's a doctor' I said in mitigation.

'He's only a feckin Houseman' she said 'He could wreck havoc in the six months he's here'.

'Should I tell Sister' I asked hoping she'd say 'leave it to me',

'Tell him first' she said 'He's the one who needs to know'.

The next time he came on the ward he went over to a patient and lifted the corner of a dressing on a gland incision on the neck and had a poke. I waited to see if he would wash his hands but he made no attempt to do so, going over to Digger Duggan's bed and picking up his chart. Quaking, I went over and stood beside him waiting, to gain his attention. His initial

'Yes, Nurse, what can I do for you' was said in abstracted way as he removed the stethoscope from around his neck to listen to the Digger's chest.

'If I could just have a minute of your time, Doctor, I said, not recognising my voice.

'Get on with it Nurse' he said, not as much as glancing in my direction.

'You have forgotten to wash your hands Doctor' I said as firmly as any seventeen years old would when confronting God.

The ensuing conversation was terse and defensive on God's side while I surprised myself with my knowledge of cross contamination, in particular staphylococcus aurous and Escherichia coli infections, and the consequences for patients, ending with

In this instance you have handled a seeping wound, came across the room and picked up a chart, pulled your stethoscope from around your neck and are about to examine this patient, all without washing your hands, Doctor'.

Two men gawping at me was too much, so scarlet from hairline to sternum I turned on my heel and left the room.

Later when I was taking the Digger's temperature he was very quiet so I apologised for the earlier confrontation

'Bejasus Nurse but the cocky little gobshoite had it coming, Heaven alone only knows where he had his hands before he came into the room' he said shuddering.

'I went and had a good scrub with carbolic to get his germs off me'.

I was immensely cheered, picked up his chart holder by the bottom edges and took it out to the sluice to disinfect it.

'Ye know an awful lot about germs Nurse' Digger said in admiration.

Ah, I smiled, if only Sr. Josephine thought the same.

By my end of month review she concluded that I did knew enough, and was technically competent enough, to be let loose with a sterile dressing trolley. I had also mastered the intricacies of many tailed bandages, T-bandages and the tension required in the herring bone technique when applying a crepe bandage. She was just about to hand back my Schedule of Nursing with several 'Proficiencies' added to my list, and a look back on my time management when she said

'Anything else you want to discuss?'

There was a look in her eye that said 'think carefully'. I remembered Tips advice about the importance of telling Sr. Josephine anything that concerned her ward before somebody else did.

It had been two weeks since the hand washing incident, and observing the Doc I had had no further cause for concern, but my gut told me she knew about it so I told the story.

'So you took it upon yourself to decide that he had become a competent and safe practitioner', she said witheringly?

I knew that *anything* I said now would dig my grave deeper. *Why hadn't I told her?*

'You also took it upon yourself to put *my* patients in jeopardy by not reporting incidents of possible cross contamination' she added?

I let her scourge me till she ran out of breath, expecting her to eventually say 'This is a matter for Matron. However she merely handed back my schedule setting out work for the next month, and indicating I could go said wryly

'Well at least your observational skills are improving'.

~ MARCH ~

Chapter 22

The month of March, heralded the arrival of three new Probationers with the improbable surnames of Sherry, Coffey and Mc Guinness. Marion Sherry, like Rita Carroll came from Monahan, Helen Coffey from Co. Cork and Kathleen Mc Guinness was from Waterford. Mc Guinness was put on St. Peter's with Tip Carroll, 'Pater' Harbourne and I. Donovan and the Mc Carthy sisters were returning to Dunmanway having finished their years training, and with good references to to ease their way up the waiting list at St. Finbarr's Hospital in Cork. Their last evening was both sad and enjoyable. Sr.Marie funded party food and Sr.Agnes moved a table into the sitting room to provide a buffet style arrangement. The Staff Nurses ran the wards between 7.00 and 9.00pm so that we could all enjoy the party. I made a little thank you speech to Theresa for her endless patience over the past two months, saying there was no way I could ever repay her.

'Ah, but there is, there is indeed' she said with mischief in her eyes.

I went up to the bedroom and removing the garment than Annie Lawlor had lovingly wrapped in tissue paper, and which had reposed in my chest of drawers since my arrival, and at Donovan's request came swanking down the stairs in the salmon pink satin dressing gown. In respect for Annie's memory I'll omit the subsequent comments and screams of hilarity, and merely say that Donovan considered she had had sweet revenge for my wear and tear on her nerves. Despite the hilarity I realised my dressing gown was a source of envy to the culchies, and had several offers to swop. Thinking of Annie's pride I couldn't bring myself to do it.

Mc Guinness was a test of tolerance both on the ward and in the Home. She inherited Donovan's bed, and from night one Corcoran and Lucey and I discovered she was a snorer. My God, could that girl snore? On the ward she was precise and methodical. Whereas I had been Donovan's shadow and never let her out of my sight she was always losing Harbourne or rather, Pater went along at her usual speed not realizing Mc Guinness was not behind her. She was a sandy haired sorrowful looking lanky girl whose wispy hair was constantly escaping from an insecurely tethered bun, and had the disconcerting habit of talking to herself, verbally reminding herself of things to do, or giving a running commentary on things somebody else was doing. Once we got used to her little quirks we discovered she had a droll sense of humour, and a good natured outlook on life, however that did not prevent her room mates wanting to kill her every night. Miraculously she had no run-ins with Sr. Bernardino for several weeks, when she did had one it was one that none of us would ever forget.

The Daughters of Charity of St. Vincent de Paul, the Order that ran the Hospital were technically not Nuns at all. Every year they took a simple personal vow of poverty, chastity and obedience while dedicating their lives to serving God. Proper Nuns took perpetual vows when they finished their noviciate dedicating their service to God for life. During my school days we used to speculate, and in some instances, hope, those nuns we hated would be missing from the ranks on the 26th March. Of course it was always wishful thinking. We mused on the same possibility now as the Feast of the Annunciation arrived. This was the day that yearly vows were renewed and while St. Patrick's Day had passed unremarked, apart from an influx of visitors, the 25th March was a day of celebration. Out-Patients was closed, all treatments cancelled, and the Sisters went off somewhere for a great congregational gathering, Blackrock, I think, leaving the Hospital in the care of the Staff Nurses and to the mercy of the Probationers. We were all on 12 hour shifts with the promise of an evening party. The day went like clockwork, everybody on their best behaviour until boredom set in mid afternoon. I knew Duffy was busy over on the Wing because she had told Tip to send me to get her if we needed her. The ambulant men on St. Peters were playing cards bemoaning the fact that there was no Racing programme for the day.

'We could have our own races' I suggested without engaging the frontal lobe of my brain.

Heads went up and eyes brightened with interest.

'OK go on then' said a delighted Malachy Hughes from the Macgillycuddy's Reeks, teased by the other patients as a 'ridire chaorach' because he was said to own a thousand sheep.

I drew the circuit which went from the front hall, down the corridor to the Private Wing, turning left and down another corridor to the laundry, through the side door, across the garden path, in through the fire door of the Chapel corridor, the final run leading back past the door of their room to the start. The laundry being closed for the day it would be easy enough to prop the side door open but the side door to the Chapel corridor was a bit more problematic because anybody using the Chapel seeing the fire door open would close it. Somebody would have to hover and open it as required. To name the participants at this point is probably reasonable, but having got away with it at the time perhaps is a mite unfair, but they know who they are. A list of runners was given to Malachy, and Fancy Finnerty a fellow enthusiast from the Curragh of Kildare assessed the form, walked the course, calculated the odds, and to prolong the fun decided on two 'horses' per race. The fastest times would then have a championship finale. News of the event had spread to the men on St. Vincent's Ward who were now sitting on the stairs, or out in the garden lining the course and waiting for the off. I did very badly in the odds, being up against a longer legged opponent, but what these culchie's didn't know was that on the Gran's dresser was a little tarnished trophy saying Bernadette Redmond; North Dublin Junior Sprinting Champion' 200 yards 1953. We had the most enormous fun for about an hour with Malachy Hughes doing a brilliant Michail O'Hehir commentary. The front door bell rang just as the champion of champions race was about to finish. In the excitement nobody answered it. We were waiting for the final sprint when Fancy had the presence of mind to look through the ornate glass panels in the door to see whose enraged finger was still on the bell. He discovered that either a giant seagull was seeking refuge, or there was a Nun on the doorstep. Common sense prevailed as he shouted a warning.

The one word 'Nun' and everybody melted away apart from the two runners who were heading straight for a confrontation with the infuriated Sister who came storming through the door taking the three internal steps at a leap. Finishing the race and well in the lead Mc Guinness must have been running with her eyes closed because she cannoned into Sr. Bernardino lifting her off her feet. Her momentum brought her down on top of her squashing the soaring head dress in the process. The runner up kept going and with a hop skip and a jump over the entangled bodies went bounding up the stairs disappearing into St. Vincent's Ward. Malachy and Fancy got C.J. to her feet and while she was too winded to speak she managed to slap their supporting arms away as she tried to adjust her starched seagull head dress.

'W-h-a-t is going on here' she croaked, her oxygen depleted lungs denying us her usual roar.

There was a moments silence as we tried to think of a believable explanation. My brain was still dealing with my unspoken rhetorical question *'What the hell is she doing here'* when Mc Guinness chimed in.

'Fire' she said, eyes wild, face red, hair streeling and cap lost somewhere along the circuit.

'Fire' responded Sr. Bernardino in incredulity with silent echo's and raised eyebrows from the rest of us.

'Yes, Sister I thought the door bell was the fire alarm so I ran to make sure fire exit was unlocked before dialling 999.

'Bedad and the doorbell went on ringing for a shocking long time altogether that it got me thinking it was the fire alarm too' Malachy said, supporting Mc Guinness.

'And you 'she said, glowering at me.

'Oh, I was evacuating the patients' I said virtuously, nodding at the patients trying to look invisible on their way back in from the garden.

'And I was helping her' Fancy said, sycophantically, not to be outdone.

I looked at Mc Guinness in admiration. Anybody who could tell a lie quicker than I could think of one was worth cultivating. Mc Guinness winning the championship's £2 prize, and her quick wittedness raised her status no end, but her snoring continued to disrupt our sleep.

'Get it right' Pat Harbourne, her mentor, snapped at her crossly when the fuss had died down. 'Don't show me up, *'if you do hear a feckin fire alarm dial 999 first'*.

Speculation about Sr. Bernardino's early return was rife including the possibility that she had not renewed her vows. The latter proved to be wishful thinking, so we concluded that she had just returned to do a sneaky check up on us. The following day we all got the third degree from Sr. Josephine but nobody cracked. Or so I thought. I had only one more week left on her ward and wanting to remain in her good graces willed the days away to escape her scrutiny. Malachy Hughes, God love him, went back to his beloved Reeks to die a few months later.

~ APRIL ~

Chapter 23

Getting up before the crack of dawn on Easter Sunday brought back memories of Sr. Kevin's North William St. Church choir when the Gran and Annie Lawlor and I would set out before the streets were aired, they, to do the First Fridays Novena, and me to sing the Latin Mass. Once I was up, and on my way, I always felt quite virtuous for making the effort, and because of the Graces and Indulgences I was accumulating by not whinging about it. On this occasion it was to plamas Sr. Josephine, who, later in the day, would be assessing the progress I had made in the three months I has been on her ward before I moved on to St. Elizabeth's Ward the following day. She had asked for 'volunteers' to escort patients to the predawn Easter Vigil and I had 'put my hand up.'

In parish churches the Easter Vigil began at midnight but being a hospital chapel we were dependent on a Chaplin with parish responsibilities who arranged our service for the hour before dawn. Sitting in the darkened Chapel waiting for the Pascal candle to be lit, I was aware that this would be the last Easter several of the patients would see. As I looked at the poor wasted face of Mag O'Neill from the lakes of Roscommon, whom I had wheeled down from the ward, I was touched by her serenity and her quiet concentration as she answered the Rosary which was being said while waiting for the Vigil to begin. The ornate white candle was lit outside in the garden, torched by burning Palm leaves and carried into the unlit Chapel. The priest then took it around the forty or so of us in the congregation lighting our individual candles which we held throughout the Liturgy of the Word. We then extinguished them as the Mass of the Resurrection commenced.

As I sat there I wondered what Maggo was thinking. At thirty eight she would be leaving four young children behind, the oldest a girl of sixteen was currently taking care of the family with the aid of Maggo's aged mother, while her husband was working on building England's first motorway. Like a lot of country women of the day, embarrassment about talking to male doctors about problems 'down below', meant her cancer got a good grip before diagnosis. Cancer of the reproductive organs had the added problem of being regarded as 'dirty' in some people's eyes with a nod and a wink intimating sexual misconduct. There may have been a grain of truth in that correlation, but not on the part of the women concerned. Statistically the women we saw would be considered a low risk group, but in an era when a lot of husbands were working away from home it may be *their* promiscuity infected the women with a predisposing virus. Today, a cervical smear would probably save Maggo's life, back then, by the time they opened her up to take a look, the cancer was inoperable having spread through the wall of the womb, and into the ovaries and mesentery. Despite heavy doses of radiotherapy her prognosis was dire.

The one thing Maggo had in common with most of our patients was a belief in a merciful God and His interceding Mother. A cancer ward was like an army camp with everybody committed to the fight. Faith was like their 'General' and gave them a belief in power over their disease. It also created a positive attitude, but always with the added proviso of 'God Willing'. Every small improvement was a victory, a battle won in a war they had no choice but to fight. It seemed to me that the march of cancer was relentless, but who was I to deny anybody their hope? ' Mass cards were shown and counted as neighbours and friends 'bought' Masses, or organised prayers via such groups as the Apostleship of Prayer for their recovery. Confraternities and Sodalities were common in every Parish and had substantial followings, their members adding their prayers in their lists of 'Special Intentions for family and friends'.

Treatment of cancer was unpleasant, painful and debilitating. In that era patient's belief in an after life was also a great comfort to them, while they may have being leaving the living, they would be joining those who had gone before. However, Mag O'Neill had no intention of dying until she had sorted her kids out.

Maggo still had a vision for the future, milestones in her children's life to aim for. She was putting together a shoebox full of small mementos, which included letters to leave them to help them to remember her. She spent her time making lists for her husband and Mother, and even on this holy occasion poked me to borrow a pen. I saw her jot down 'Communion dress for Ellen'. 'Is there anything you want for yourself Maggo' I asked her later as I saw her going through her lists.

'Well, with the Grace of God, a visit to Knock, otherwise I'll have to be content with a bottle of the Holy Water' she said with a wan smile.

I had only known Maggo a few weeks but she was a patient to remember. She never complained. Every morning and evening she had to climb on to a treatment chair in the lithotomy position where she sat with her feet in stirrups to have a vaginal peroxide wash out. Duffy made this treatment matter of fact by just pulling the screen around the chair in the treatment room and getting on with it, whereas Sr. Josephine went through the usual dance of the seven veils and when she was actually doing the douching Probationers were not allowed to participate for modesty reasons. Apart from the welfare of her children Maggo's main concern was the putrid smell from the vaginal discharge she was experiencing. Was it noticeable? How would she manage it at home? Duffy came to the rescue by finding some vaginal douche equipment and showing her how to use it. Maggo winked at me. 'I wonder did she ever have the need for it' she said slyly. 'If I'd had the use of one of these I can bet you I wouldn't be a mother of four'.

I only had a vague idea what she was talking about, pregnancy prevention being against the law of God and State. A few days later laden with sanitary towels and pain relief she was sent home to await the outcome of the radium treatment. She died from a massive haemorrhage in the ambulance on the journey. 'Merciful God, my arse' I thought as I wept for her. I didn't think much of his Holy Mother either. One of my last memories of Mag O'Neill was her sweet voice singing at the Easter Mass;

Hail Queen of Heaven
The Ocean Star
Guide of the wanderer here below.
Thrown on life's surge
We claim thy care
Save us from peril and from woe.

I know Maggo believed in the joys of everlasting life, but you'd think the 'Blessed Virgin' might have interceded to let her see her children one last time before death claimed her.

Chapter 24

'Will youze for Gawd's sake give over about germ's' said an irate Bernie Moran.

Six of us had met up in Fortes in O'Connell Street to share Knickerbocker Glories and Melancholy Babies. In the three months since I had left Summerhill there had been big changes in my life, not matched in the friends I had left behind. The girls, Bridie Fitz, Mary Bennett, and Bernie's main topic of conversation was Grace Kelly's forthcoming marriage while the Hemplestall boys and Paddy Duffy were excited by Teddy boy fashion and Bill Haley's 'Rock around the Clock' playing on the jukebox. My contribution to the conversation was my American pen pal and a newly acquired knowledge of bacteriology. I took all the joy out of the occasion by asking the sundae maker how long his scoop makers had been in the cloudy jug of water, then watched in disgust as he stuck the triangular wafers in the ice cream with his fingers having just been biting his fingernails. Noting the grubbiness of the dish cloth the waitress used to wipe our table I listed the possible illnesses we could end up with.

'Yiz are turnin me stumik' Bridie Fitz said glaring at me.

This put a stop to my intended lecture on contamination and the amount of germs we were ingesting. I also didn't think that the boys would be interested in the fact that there were nearly three hundred types of germs living in the mouth of a human being. Most of those germs are harmless, but when two people kiss, thousands of germs flow from one mouth to the other, and while saliva produces enzymes for self-defence the thought of the exchange of germs somewhat took the shine off kissing at the time. A couple of lectures in the College of Surgeons and two sessions in the Pathology Dept had turned me into a germ phobic.

My first session in Pathology was spent with a keen young lab technician who took me around a Ward at Mercer's Hospital nearby, and let me loose with Pietri agar dishes and sterile swabs to check for contamination on common surfaces. I swabbed toilet chains, seats, taps, door handles, several items in the sluice room, and then my own skin, hands, nose and apron. A few days later I returned to look at the results under a microscope. It was truly a revelation, a hidden seething jungle made visible, and teeming with pathogens. Not only where the inanimate objects covered in germs, I was a walking, talking living mass of pathogens too and should have been going around with a bell, and a sign around my neck reading 'Unclean, Unclean.' To make my day he then showed me a film of billions of bed mites, invisible to the naked eye but keeping me, and you, company in our nice warm beds. Those sessions brought back childhood memories of holidays in Co. Galway. There was no inside sanitation in my Granny's house down the bog so I have no recollection of ever washing my hands after 'doing my business', a factor no doubt, in conjunction with drinking untreated milk and water and visits to Bina Lenihan's kitchen that resulted in a hardiness that set me up for life. Bina was my mother's cousin whose lack of hygiene was legendry. She always looked well scrubbed but never thought to change her wrap around apron, or clean anything. She had a pub where the snug was only swept when a regular would take a broom to the trekked in mud or manure from the yard outside that prevented him standing in a favourite spot. The bar was sticky from previous slops, but Bina was always generous if your glass stuck to the counter causing you any spillage. Glasses were dunked in a bucket of water to rinse them, but the bucket was often not emptied for days. However the mould covered tea towels probably produced enough Penicillin to counteract the bacteria in the water. The kitchen was nearly as bad and we were strictly forbidden by my Aunt May, my mother's sister with whom we spent our long summer holidays, from letting food or drink pass our lips when we went to visit. We regarded this as very unreasonable so took no notice whatsoever and enjoyed many a fig roll and red lemonade around Bina's kitchen table as we competed to roll old dough and cigarette ash into balls.

My Ma, God rest her, was equally fastidious, making judicious use of the loofah and fine tooth comb to ensure that her children enjoyed a high standard of cleanliness. Despite the pair of them I had enjoyed a care free childhood with no fear of germs but I could now see myself turning into a hygiene freak and I wondered if I would if I would ever set foot in Bina's again. I was also aware of a gulf opening between my friends and me and didn't know what to do about it. It wasn't just caused by our diverging interests but the fact that we had no access to telephones and that my off duty was liable to be changed at short notice. By the end of the year I only saw them in passing. The Pathology sessions also gave me an insight into Sr. Josephine's annoyance with my not informing her of the Houseman's attitude to cross infection. He was not going to learn anything from me castigating him; I should have gone straight to her.

Chapter 25

St Elizabeth's Ward was a sixteen bedded ward on the first floor. To the right of the main staircase it was the main female public ward with another ten beds in smaller rooms for Skin patients. The latter were flexibly used when there were no Dermatology patients to fill them. Sr. Apolline was the Nun in charge but was currently on night duty, so the Ward was being run by a young Nun, Sr. Catherine, who was filling in time waiting for the new Children's Hospital in Crumlin to open. Sr. Vincent from the men's ward across the landing kept an eye on us but the mainstay for running the Ward to Sr. Apolline's standards was Sheila Moran a Staff Nurse, originally from Tralee. Sheila had trained in Manchester and had worked there for thirty years, acquiring a Mancunian accent and varicose veins. Raven haired when young she now dyed it a glossy jet black, but never did it frequently enough, so some weeks a half inch of grey showed in her centre parting. Her one fault was that we were reminded half a dozen times a day how far we fell below the standards of the 'MRI'.

'If the Manchester Royal Infirmary is such a feckin wonderful hospital what's she doing back here' an irate and red faced Bina Corcoran said through gritted teeth having been criticised about the generous size of the cotton wool balls she was making for autoclaving.

Bina and I and the new Probationer Helen Coffee were Sheila's minions. Apart from her annoying comparisons she was fair minded and efficient. Sr. Catherine beneath her 18th Century habit was a skinny red head in her early twenties with nice regular features. She probably had little or no experience managing a ward, or looking after patients with cancer. We didn't know what to make of her. In theory she was supposed to be responsible for overseeing my training for the next three months because Moran didn't have the authority to sign off any 'Proficiencies' in my Schedule. This was ridiculous since she had a quarter of a century's more experience than Sr. Catherine, who, if she wasn't a nun, would be a very junior Staff Nurse in comparison. In preparation for giving injections I had waded through the relevant muscular skeletal and nervous system Chapters in my Anatomy and Physiology book and had prepared syringes and drawn up the medication and observed intramuscular and subcutaneous injections being given. I could do it blindfold but had been putting off asking for a proficiency assessment. I had practiced with sterile water on a pillow and a loaf of bread. The best thing to practice on was an orange but they were few and far between. The thought of piercing a patient's skin and going straight through her sciatic nerve was terrifying so to put an end to my dithering Moran told me in no uncertain terms that I was next to useless since I could not give injections, test urine or administer enemas, and was not pulling my weight. She obviously had a 'word' with Sr. Catherine who suddenly developed a burning desire to go through my Schedule with me. By the end of the day we were back in Sheila's good books when I said I was ready for assessment.

  I don't know which of us. Sr. Catherine or I was the most nervous the following morning when Moran gave me a list of injections to give. We were not yet in the age of disposable syringes so glass syringes, plungers and needles had to be boiled in the sterilizer and put together with sterile forceps and placed in individual sterile containers once the medication had been drawn up. God, the palaver, I had done this more than a dozen times, but under observation, my hands were shaking so much it took me three times as long. Trying to remember the five 'R's I checked through all the injections silently one more time; right patient, right drug, right dose, right route and right time.

'Who do you want to do first' Sr. Catherine asked? Decisions decisions, somebody fat or somebody thin, a viscous liquid hard to inject, or an easier one? 'Let's just do the round as usual' I volunteered. 'Don't let them know it's your first time' she murmured. Yeh right! I knew every eye in the ward was on me as I approached the first bed and pulled the curtains. Edith Keogh had been a hefty woman before her colon cancer had ravaged her, but she still had a good size haunch which she now exposed for me to inject. Unfortunately it was an oily Vitamin K injection which needed a big needle and slow dispersal. How I managed it I'll never know, but it gave me the confidence to continue until all injections had been done and I was signed off as proficient. Corcoran confessed that she had told the women I was being assessed so I went around and thanked them. Edith told me she nearly died of fright when she realized she was first on my list 'but I knew the good Lord was with us when you made the sign of the cross on my bum'. I didn't tell the poor woman that that was not a sign of piety but to show Sr. Catherine that I was identifying the upper outer quadrant of her buttock to avoid the sciatic nerve.

~May ~

Chapter 26

The month of May turned Northbrook Road into an avenue of mature verdant greens and coppery purple with an impressive tree planted on the pavement outside every residence. Hedges and front gardens along the road were bursting with smaller flowering trees. The apple and cherry blossom were past their best but the acacias, lilacs and Magnolias were at their most glorious. In comparison Gran's row of geraniums and herbs along the balcony looked sad. It was my fortnightly day off and I was off home for the afternoon. In the Nurses Home the one concession to days off and late shifts was that you were allowed to have breakfast between nine and ten. To entice you out of bed you could have a boiled egg and toast instead of porridge, but even that didn't move some of us before mid day. We seldom got Sunday as a day off because if the patient's had visitors they were likely to come on the Sabbath, thereby creating more work. Also, for some reason Ward Sisters, Nuns or not, decided in days beyond memory, that despite God creating it as a day of rest, Sunday was cleaning, auditing and ordering day.

Today was a special occasion. My Aunt Tess age 31 was engaged and getting married in September. I had yet to meet *the fiancée* who would be at the Gran's for tea. Tommy turned out to be a 36 year old stocky man from Leitrim with receding sandy hair, and if I could bore for Ireland on germs, Tommy could do it on any subject under the sun. Tea went well with Sheila turning up to join in in preparations for the big event. Instead of taking himself off to a local saloon Tommy ensconced himself behind the Sunday paper in Granda's captain's chair over by the window, something no self respecting Dublin man would do, while the four of us sat around the table with the Gran replenishing tea cups. I listened as plans were made for the happy couple to move to a cottage off Bella Street. The date set for the wedding, 11th September, was disclosed and choices of venue for the reception were down to two.

'Who's your bridesmaid' I asked, not overtly interested as I helped myself to a slice of Fuller's walnut cake.

Three pair of eyes looked at me in astonishment, before saying in unison

'*You* are of course'.

At least half a dozen sins of blasphemy flashed across my mind, but my look of horror must have said it all. Amidst the cacophony of four people talking at once, and accusations of base ingratitude from Sheila, I felt I was about to topple into the Ninth Circle of Hell. I wracked my brain trying to think of more worthy, willing and meritorious candidates and came up with at least three who were dismissed by Sheila as too fat, too small and too stupid and anyway it had to be me because I would be in charge of the page boy and flower girl, aka her children. My heart went out to them and I wondered if they had been told?

'No, because they would be sick with excitement' Sheila said with certainty. Sick, yes. Excitement, I don't think so.

I realised that rebellion was futile and that I was not going to get out of this 'honour' so thought I'd better do it with good grace. It was at this point that Gran administered the coup de grâce.

'When are you free to go shopping' she asked.

No, no, no, no, no. I-was -not –going- shopping.

I reminded Tess that May Grant was a great dressmaker and would give her what was wanted at a good price. The Gran's eyes lit up, but not in agreement, it was the light of battle, and this time she had might on her side. No department store floor walker was going to turn down rigging out a wedding. I lost the will to live when colour schemes were discussed and got up to go.

I went across the hall to see Annie Lawlor on my way out. She was waiting for the others to leave before going over to spend the evening with Gran.

'What did yiz make of yer man' she asked with mischief in her voice.

'Well, he's not exactly God's gift' I responded cautiously.

That was enough for Annie. On went the kettle, out came the Baby Power's 'to warm the cockles', the front door was closed to alert us to any interruptions and the slagging session began. Both Annie and I were in agreement that it should be a mortal sin to bore people, and that all bores should be consigned to the fiery furnaces of hell. Not because of the boring per se but because of the murderous thoughts they raised in good hearted people. And last but not least Annie was of the opinion that Tess would rue the day she married a culchie. From my seventeen year old perspective I wondered why they were getting married at all at their age; surely they'd had their life. Hadn't they? Tommy and Tess were coming up to celebrating their fortieth wedding anniversary before her death in 1995. Their formula for a long and happy marriage seemed to be that he talked and she ignored him.

Chapter 27

Giving an enema is easy. I had watched it being done several times and had no real qualms about being assessed. I had the trolley set, the commode by the side of the bed, Renee Mc Grath on her left side, with left knee bent, one pillow under her head and the foot of the bed slightly raised. A covered pitcher with 2ozs of liquid soap in a quart of warm water was ready to have its temperature checked before being poured into an 8oz container with a large bore lubricated rectal tube attached. The enema would be dispensed slowly 8ozs at a time. All I had to do was expel air from the tube, insert it a good six inches up her bum, and release the clamp. My Practical Nursing Manual said that for an enema to be successful the patient must be psychologically prepared, the solution properly diluted and dissolved, the right size tubing selected, temperature between 105-110 degrees, given slowly holding the container twelve inches above the bed, stopping to allow cramping to pass but persevering until the full amount was given. All boxes checked, including the fact that the Renee had had several enemas in the past, enemas being de rigour before you gave birth and Renee had done so five times.

So what could go wrong? Well for a start there was an unforeseen problem not mentioned in manuals. I am left handed so with the patient on her left side I was on the wrong side of the bed. I would have to insert the tube with my right hand, control the clamp with my right hand and replenish the solution ditto. Sr. Catherine smiled reassuringly, talking away to Renee to take her mind off the ham-fisted idiot behind her. I managed to expel the air, insert the tube and open the clamp without too much difficulty but pouring from the pitcher was problematic. It was heavy and my hand shook spilling a little on the floor when I was transferring the solution to the 8oz container. However the quart went in ounce by ounce, and Renee, bless her, was holding on to it when disaster struck.

We heard Matrons voice from the other side of the curtains doing one of her 'surprise' Ward rounds. Sr. Catherine went on automatic pilot and instead of helping the patient out of bed to the commode pulled the top sheet taut and tucked it under the mattress imprisoning her. The desperate woman rolled over to get out my side of the bed stepping in the spilt soap solution as she did so, bringing herself and me down in a heap on the floor. Sr. Catherine was nano seconds too late with the commode. There was an explosion as a quart of green soap solution and a colon full of brown slurry covering me, Renee and the floor. We watched in horror as it crept out under the curtains. Matron was certainly not practicing *'Custody of the Eyes'* that day.

Later when I took my Schedule to Sr. Catherine to sign she told me I'd better do one more to confirm my competence, or incompetence, as the case may be. I pointed out to her that if she had not tucked in the bed clothes the disaster would never have happened, and despite the unorthodox ending the enema had been a success. Renee agreed, 'I feel stones lighter' she said happily. Sr. Catherine signed me off, primarily I think, because she didn't want to be anywhere near to me when I gave another enema.

By comparison testing urine was fraught with danger but that assessment was incident free. Well almost. In the fifties urine testing involved Bunsen burners, mentholated spirit lamps and various chemical compounds. It was carried out in a well lit area in the sluice room which had its own bench top and locked cupboard, the latter in case we had any suicidal or alcoholic patients, or nurses, on the ward. There was also a fire extinguisher on the wall in the unlikely event of setting fire to your self, or causing an explosion.

Sr. Catherine looked decidedly nervous at being in close proximity to me and this potentially lethal cocktail and stood well back as I struck a match to ignite the Bunsen burner. The urine samples in glass containers were in a neat row all labelled with a list for the results to be recorded

Name
Collection time
Test time
Appearance
Smell
Specific gravity
Ph; acid / alkali
Protein
Blood
Glucose

With my line of testing solutions and test tubes on the bench in front of me I started, explaining the mysteries of Tincture of Guaiacum, Ozonic Ether, Benedict's Solution and Acetic Acid as I went along. I was actually well used to testing urine since it was a job Donovan had hated doing so had let me do it with minimal supervision. I had cleared everything away and was just about to hand my Schedule to Sr. Catherine when I remembered Donovan's training. 'When you're being assessed look to see that the fire extinguishers safety check is not out of date'. Well, better late than never. Last checked; 23/3/53.

Dear God. Should I mention it?

Of course I shouldn't, but being a smart arse I did.

Sr. Catherine unhooked it and gave it a shake. 'It sounds empty she said pressing the nozzle.

Oh my God! How could so much foam be in such a small container? I know knew what Donovan meant about being cursed, and felt like telling the Holy Sister to go down to the Chapel and bless herself with Holy Water or say an Act of Contrition, or both.

~ June ~

Chapter 28

Six months into my training I knew very little about anatomy and physiology apart from illustrations in books. I had a programme of lectures and practical demonstrations that I could attend at Mercer's Hospital or the College of Surgeons but being the only Probationer to start in January I often felt too intimidated to do so alone. However now that Coffee, Sherry and Mc Guinness were coming along behind me it was an incentive to keep my head start. Of those Probationers ahead of me several had still not attended an obligatory post mortem, so with medical students busy with exams and re sits, four of us went off, two straight from night duty, to spend a morning with a pathologist. He was obviously more used to dealing with rowdy medical students so we got his mandatory sermon on respect for, and dignity of, the dead. We were a select little group of six, two being young student nurses from Mercer's, who had probably not yet seen a dead body, and four of us even younger who dealt with death frequently. While they still had to come to terms with the fact that patients die, we were overjoyed if they lived. The autopsy room was clinical, and spacious enough, to contain an examination table and three trolleys with shrouded forms. The overpowering smell was of Formaldehyde with an undertone of a butchers shop on a hot day. There are two smells a nurse never forgets Formaldehyde and Paraldehyde.

We gathered around the first table. The initial shock of the Autopsy Technician making an incision from ear to ear, around the base of the skull, and pulling the skin forward and down over the forehead before sawing the crown off the head, rooted me to the spot. I was afraid to look at anybody in case I joined them in a dead faint, or a projectile vomiting fest in the big stainless steel sink where the Pathologist was scrubbing up. However we were all still standing, if a bit green around the gills when he approached the table and that literally was the worst of it. The fascination of seeing a body in three dimensions took over. And it was a body, a male body, and that was all it was. It was not a person, or a patient, but a waxwork like caricature of the name label tied on the toe. For the first time ever I understood the Irish habit of calling a dead body 'the remains'. We saw what self indulgence could do on the first body's lungs and liver, the second body, a woman, showed the ravages of cancer of the uterus and mesenteric glands, and I thought of poor Mag O'Neill. The third body was an ancient toothless old crone of a granny well into her eighties, with an address in the Monto whose poverty stricken diet of bread and tea had crumbled her bones, and whose brain looked like Emmental cheese as a result of dementia. The Pathologist, with an attentive audience, dissected organ after organ for us to examine until we reluctantly left at mid day. I went back to my Anatomy and Physiology Manual with renewed interest, and a much better idea about the size and situation of human organs. Having completed the Autopsy experience I had now progressed to a level where I could lay out a patient under supervision. Now there was something to look forward to …

Chapter 29

The 'Skins' on the Ward kept to themselves and were housed in two four bedded rooms and one two bedded. They were seldom admitted for more than a fortnight, usually for intensive treatment of psoriasis. On arrival they were sometimes unrecognizable with scaly inflamed swollen skin and maddened to tears by the urge to scratch. Dermatological treatments were pretty basic; Antibiotics to control underlying infection, coal tar paste to relieve rash and inflammation and soften plaques, and then Lassar's paste instead of soap to wash off coal tar and moisturize the skin. Ultra violet treatment was used as the condition improved and coal tar paste was reduced and Lassar's paste was left on the skin to moisten any remaining plaques. Acute flare-ups of eczema were treated in a similar way.

Because of the nature of the treatment these patients had dark coloured sheets which were changed and bagged every day. The amount of dead skin was quite phenomenal and what wasn't shed in the bed was sloughed of in the bath. To forget to put the filter in the plughole when you let the water out was sufficient to get you sent to Matrons office to have the cost of a plumber deducted from your salary. The rooms reeked of the smell of coal tar which I quite liked. I found great satisfaction looking after skin patients. Their swift recovery was a testament to good nursing care. They were also appreciative and thankful that they were going home to live with chronic conditions, unlike their neighbours in the big ward whose conditions were progressively deadly.

Not being used to any excitement in the Skin's rooms the palaver that took place a few days after the fire extinguisher incident was completely unforeseen. We were expecting a patient from Laois, so when we were told the ambulance had arrived Sr. Catherine went down to the Basement entrance to meet it. Sr. Bernardino was already there having seen the ambulance pull up, and officious as ever had taken control. A timid well shrouded little woman, sitting in a wheel chair was handed over to Sr. Catherine. The patient's small suitcase along with a brown folder containing records, were placed on the patients lap by the crew. Ascending in the lift Sr. Catherine wheeled the patient to the two bedded room and asked if I could 'clerk her in'

'Sorry Sister, I can't' I said. 'I'm not allowed to admit a patient until I've been assessed'

A glint of amusement came into her eye

'I may be from Cork, Redmond but I'm not stupid. I'd rather stick pins in my eyes than do another assessment with you' she said with fervour.

Aha, shades of Donovan there I thought. If only she had done my assessment there and then she could have saved herself a lot of explaining an hour later.

'Nurse will put you to bed Mrs. Sweeney and will make you a nice cup of tea' she said smiling reassuringly at a puzzled looking patient.

I pulled the curtains around one of the two beds in the unoccupied room and allowed Mrs. Sweeney to undress and settle in. On my return the curtains were pulled back and the tea trolley having done its round Mrs. Sweeney was sitting by her bed drinking tea and shedding skin everywhere. I explained the Ward layout and routine to her but she seemed totally bemused by it all. Establishing that she wasn't deaf I thought the journey had tired her out so left her in peace.

Moran went off duty at 5.00pm leaving Sr. Catherine nominally in charge with Sr. Vincent keeping an eye on us from the men's ward across the landing. A few minutes after Moran's departure the phone rang. Helen Coffee was nearest to it so answered, listened, and said

'Thank you' Sister'.

'That was Sr. Marie, Mrs. Sweeney has arrived' she informed us.

My immediate reaction was 'She's wandered downstairs' and ran to have a look in her room, but there she was, lying on her bed, dozing away. Sr. Catherine was numb with shock when she discovered the name on the records accompanying the patient we had admitted did not contain the word 'Sweeney', that she was from Co. Kildare not Co. Laois and was a 'Prodlsan' not a 'Catlick'. A minute of total panic followed before she took charge.

'Coffee, go down and bring up Mrs. Sweeney and put her in the empty bed in the four bedder and make sure she has tea and is put on the supper list'.

'Get Sr. Vincent, and then guard that woman with your life until we find out where she is supposed to be' she ordered me.

Sr. Vincent was a calm amiable gentle person, the kind you want to shake in an emergency. I felt like dragging her across the landing as I tried to explain to her how we had acquired an extra patient. In the meantime Sr. Catherine had been reading the records and found a letter acknowledging a Mrs. H's admission to the City of Dublin Skin and Cancer Hospital in Hume St. the other side of Stephen's Green.

Sr. Marie was summoned to discuss practicalities.

Facts; Sr. Bernardino (much glee) had accepted the patient; the patient was only technically in our care, but was most definitely in one of our beds, ergo, how was she to be got to Hume St.? Sr. Marie balked at hiring an ambulance for such a short distance. A cab was a possibility, but who was sensible enough to accompany her. All three nuns looked dubiously at me.

'Why can't she go in the ambulance down stairs' Coffee enquired brightly? 'The ambulance men are having their sandwiches so they haven't moved off yet' she continued.

As Probationers we were always been told not to run, but Sr. Marie took the stairs like a greyhound, and I had the feeling she would have slid down the elegant banister if it had got her to the hall a split second earlier. Sure enough the Kildare ambulance was still there, and while Sr. Marie charmed the crew with newly brewed tea in lieu of their flask, Sr. Catherine and I bundled Mrs. H into a wheelchair, repacked her case and had her ready to go when the tea was consumed. Sr. Bernardino was nowhere to be seen, but profuse apologies from everybody else accompanied Mrs. H. on her way.

'I did wonder why you kept calling me Mrs. Sweeney' she said looking at me accusingly 'but I didn't like to say anything'.

Ye Gods! How long would that have gone on if the real Mrs. Sweeney hadn't turned up?

'Get your cloak Nurse; you'd better go with her' Sr. Marie told me.

It was only a ten minute journey but my mind raced with all the disasters that could befall Mrs. H in that short space of time. They might as well have sent the Lady of Shalott with her because I was just as cursed.

Sitting up front between them once we had delivered Mrs. H, I was by now on first name terms with the crew, one of whom, Con, was trying to persuade me to go dancing.

'Let me hear what the bell sounds like' I pleaded.

Blues and two's it was not, but it was still an ear shattering sound, and attracted a passing Garda car as we came up to the lights on

Stephens Green to turn left into Leeson Street. I learned later that the 'Alert' as it was called, with its single rotating blue light, was strictly for emergency situations. If I had not been reared on Summerhill I would have been shocked to the core by the language emanating from Jim, the ambulance driver, as the Garda car drove up beside us. The Guard in the passenger seat wound down his window

'Where are ye going' he asked in a machine gun Cork accent?

Being from Kildare they hadn't a clue.

'Holles St' I said off the top of my head remembering the hospital of my birth.

'Yer on the wrong side of the Green' he told us.

Then turning on *his* 'Alert' said helpfully

'Follow us'.

We did a circuit of Stephen's Green, went back through Hume Street where we had dropped off Mrs. H; then into Ely Place and Lower Merrion Street and eating up Fenian Street we headed for the side entrance of Holles Street National Maternity Hospital. A blaspheming ambulance crew, and a nurse, praying insincerely to a Deity who was probably too busy to listen, arrived at the side entrance. 'Please let them drive on' I repeated over and over, as I watched for the indicator signal on the Garda car which would show their intention. In between these exhortations I wondered what the penalty was for lying to the Garda Síochána. Much to our relief as we pulled up their left indicator went on as they gave us a wave and proceeded on their way. We still had to explain away an empty ambulance to the midwife who came rushing out with a wheel chair. The dance date with Con never materialized. I think he figured out I was cursed.

~ JULY ~

Chapter 30

At the end of June when I went into Sr. Marie's office to sign for my salary I noticed it had been rounded up to £5.10s. 0d. Written on the little brown envelope the explanation said 'Reimbursement of Board and Lodging 1st – 7th July £2.7.s 6d.

'What does that mean' I asked.

'Well, since you won't be here, your board for the week is added to your salary.

'Where will I be' I asked, not unreasonably.

'Well, at home I assume, unless you have other plans, she said.

Before I had time to take this in, the glow of charity reached her eyes

'Of course you can stay here if you want to' the Lady Almoner Sr. Marie said, to be quickly subjugated by the Bursar Sr. Marie who added

'I'd have to take back the £2.7s.6d.'

'Why won't I be here' I asked still none the wiser.

She looked at me as if I was acting the maggot.

'You'll be on holiday' she said slowly as one does when talking to a dopey teenager.

'You *do* know that you have a week's holiday' she continued, annunciating every word, with emphasis on the 'do'.

No, I did not know that I had a week's holiday. No, nobody told me I had a week's holiday, No; I was not expecting a week's holiday, as the average time we were rewarded with a holiday was at the nine month milestone.

I went back to the ward to seek an explanation and got short shrift from Moran who pointed out 'that while she might *run* the ward she was not *in charge* of the ward so to seek redress elsewhere. Sr. Catherine was more apologetic but took no responsibility for the decision, or for letting me know.

'I thought Moran would tell you' she said.

I had some sympathy for Moran in this instance, so decided to stop whinging and make plans. Bina Corcoran was two months senior to me and still hadn't had a holiday. When I found her in the sluice room she looked mightily guilty when I told her I was off the following week.

'I know' she said going as red as her hair, 'it should have been me'.

'Why are you not going' I asked, puzzled?

'I'd need to be feckin mad to go home in the middle of harvest she explained emphatically ; 'My Mam would work me like a slave in the house, and my Dada and brothers would have me out in the fields any spare minute I had'.

Ah, ha, now while Jackeens didn't have to worry about harvests I had to worry about a demented Granny determined to escort me to every dress shop and department store in Dublin intent on purchasing a pink bridesmaids dress, with matching shoes. Decisions, decisions, why was life always so full of decisions? Harvest in Galway with my late Ma's family, or a shopping marathon in Dublin with the Gran, two aunts and two mutinous young cousins? No contest.

Saturday saw me on the train to Galway with memories of St. Elizabeth Ward already fading before we reached the Curragh, and as we chugged through Tullamore, Athlone, Ballinasloe and Athenry guilt about the Grans gnashing of teeth receded in line with the railway track we were passing over. By the time we reached Oranmore my mind was full of many long happy childhood summers I had spent in the next Parish the townlands of my ancestors engraved on my memory, Gortcloonmore, Claregalway and Cregboy, my current destination. I was met at Oranmore by Uncle Mick and his youngest child, Johnny. With a new horse, but the same old cart, and Uncle Mick telling me time after time how very welcome I was we clipped clopped along. Trotting through Carnmore and down into Cregboy the village school and Church at Claregalway crossroads came into view, and I knew a left turn would see us home and to Aunt May crying on the doorstep. No matter what the occasion you could depend on Aunt May to cry.

A week of hay making in good weather and my pale Celtic skin reddened, burned, peeled and freckled. Scratched feet and frazzled hair was witness to my hay making efforts which I discovered I was useless at. The hay was forked up to me on top of a hay rick, but I found I couldn't balance *and* gather in the hay with my bare feet at the same time. I also kept up a constant whinge about the thorns and nettles among the hay.

'Sure the Mammy Baboon in the Dublin eZoo would do a better job for a bloody banana, *and* keep her gob shut' a neighbouring farmer quipped in exasperation.

Pat Cullinan was the same farmer who had accused me of killing the local Canon years before; another time, another story, same curse. His mother Molly had seen me through my Gaelic Viva for a Scholarship Exam for secondary school and still insisted on talking to me in Irish to keep me up to scratch. A month hence, in the middle of the corn harvest, she had a stroke and was dead within three days. Because of my ineptitude at rick stacking I was relegated to churning butter and making the tea, joining my cousin Bridgie in the task of feeding the ever hungry and parched workforce. Our only reward was the price of two tickets for Hanley's Hall for the ubiquitous cowboy film at the weekend, which we saw to the end despite the reel breaking twice and ending up in pandemonium with the actor's voices totally out of synch. One of my most enjoyable memories during the week was an afternoon spent in Bina Lenihan's kitchen. Deciding that the hydrochloric acid in my stomach would be a match for Bina's collation I enjoyed what was on offer. After all, the Moore children had survived living with Bina for nearly a decade, their young mother, Delia, having succumbed to the ravages of cancer at the time. Delia had been my godmother and had died within three months of my own mother so Bina's kitchen was a place of happy childhood memories. The familiar smell of peat, porter, ammonia and damp clothes wafted through from the snug. Back at Aunt May's I looked her straight in the eye, and as of old, denied that any food or drink had passed my lips; Bridgie leaving the room to avoid complicity.

With £1 in my pocket from a weeping Aunt May, and laden with poultry and farm produce for the family, I was met at Kingsbridge Station in Dublin by Christy who relieved me of my burden while I tipped the Guard for his help in festooning me with seeping brown paper parcels of poultry and leaking shoe boxes containing eggs and butter. I made straight for the Nurses Home to get ready for an early start the next morning. I had bought copies of the Cork Examiner and the Connacht Tribune for the women in the big ward who fought over them with delight. I had also brought back a jam jar full of aromatic newly turned hay which was passed from bed to bed for them to smell. So much pleasure for such a small outlay; as on every seasonal occasion I wondered how many of the sixteen would be alive to see another harvest. Later on I told them about my hay making efforts and about a childhood drama concerning jam jars. 'You should write all that down' one of them said' Aye, the world is changing so fast all this will all soon be history 'added another. Too true, but it took me more than fifty years to take their advice.

Throughout the summer months a polio outbreak raged in Co. Cork which, by August, had turned anybody with a Cork accent into a pariah. Admissions from Cork were cancelled and visitors forbidden. Probationers were allowed to go home at their own risk, but had to return with a medical certificate saying they had not been in contact with the disease. The letter was meaningless because the majority of infected contacts recovered, undiagnosed, having exhibited mild symptoms only. For the people of Cork, catching the disease was their primary fear, but a close second was the possibility of missing the All Ireland Finals, football against Galway, and hurling against Wexford, both to be held in Croke Park. The GAA solution was to postpone the matches to the latter end of September hoping the colder weather would by then have killed off the virus. I have no idea what the Department of Health stance was, or whether it was left to Dev and John Charles to make a decision, but I know it went down like a lead balloon in the Dwellings, which was enroute of the walking thousands on their way to Croke Park. While the Gran was all for sprinkling them with Holy Water, Annie Lawlor was of a mind to spray them with undiluted Jeyes Fluid.

Chapter 31

The rest of July passed with the women enjoying what fine weather we had out in the garden. The voices of the children laughing and playing in the garden of No.5 drifted over the wall. Miss Carr's Children Home sounded a happy place and brought the sounds of everyday life into the quietness of the Hospital garden. The scorched skin of those having radium treatment meant sitting in the sun was out of the question but there was sufficient shade to keep the Radiologist happy. The Radiotherapy Department were also very picky about the use of talcum powder, mentholated spirit and scented soap which made the 'back' round a nightmare.

We had two deaths on the ward both of whom I had laid out, the first under supervision with Sr. Vincent and the second accompanied by Coffee. After the morning of post mortems I had no fear of dead bodies and felt privileged to be able to perform 'the last offices'. Both patients had not long been admitted so because I had had no personal investment in nursing them, I was not upset by their deaths.

'Lay Mrs. out Nurse as her family would want to remember her' Sr. Vincent had told me.

'Won't the undertaker do that I asked?

'There's a lot can happen between now and the undertakers parlour' she reminded me acerbically,' 'including the fact her two brothers are on their way here expecting to view the body'.

With no more to be said, I closed Mrs's F's eyes and set to and washed her from head to toe, and while still observing the rules of modesty pressed down on her lower abdomen to void any urine still in her bladder. I dried her hair, cleaned out her nose, put her dentures in and cutting a slit in a length of gauze bandage put her chin through the slit lifting her bottom jaw and tied this sling on top of her head to keep her mouth closed. This produced a half smile on her face so Sr. Vincent had me loosen the sling to produce a bit more gravitas. I preferred my version, but hers prevailed. The necessary, but undignified part came next. To prevent seepages from the body, I packed her rectum with toe, a cheap form of cotton wool and raised her head on a pillow to prevent any expanding internal contents from purging. If there had been any possibility of discharge from her vagina I would have packed that orifice as well. I trimmed and cleaned her nails, combed and styled her hair and dressed her body in a white paper backless gown. She was then transferred to the mortuary trolley for a final 'tidy up'. Gown straightened, hands clasped in repose with rosary beads intertwined between her fingers and two pennies on her eyes to keep them closed. A gauze bandage enclosed her ankles to keep her legs straight, and finally a label containing name, date of birth, and hospital number was attached to her toe. This had to be double checked by a trained member of staff which made me wonder if there had been some Sweeney moments between the undertakers. Covered in a sheet and purple canopy she was removed to the mortuary where my main responsibility on handing over the body was to return to the ward carrying a pillow to replace the one under the head of Mrs F. Pillows were always in short supply which resulted in periodic pillow rustling raids between Wards.

Deaths of patients I had looked after was harder to cope with. The women, unlike the men, mostly went home to die, so we dreaded Sr. Marie bringing up any post addressed to 'The Nursing Staff, Elizabeth Ward'. We would scrutinize the post mark trying to guess who it was from, and what news it contained while waiting for Moran to open it. Sometimes the news would be good, a letter from a patient saying she was battling on 'thanks, be to God', but more often, a memorial card from a member of the family, or a notification of a Mind Mass to let us know a patient had died. For patients on the ward it was a blow if somebody they had drawn support from on previous admissions had lost the fight. The list of the dead was added to the Book of Remembrance in the Chapel to remind us to include them in our prayers. Nowadays everybody is offered all kinds of 'support and counselling' and there are bookshelves full of books dealing with death and bereavement, body image and psychic trauma,' There is also a whole new specialism in the provision of palliative and terminal care, but we just nursed with love and grieved in our own way. It helped that death was not tucked away behind screens but part of the fabric of day to day life on the Ward, and that we were able to reminisce about patients we had nursed.

Around this time a letter arrived for me addressed to St. Peter's Ward. I went down to Sr. Josephine's Office to pick it up, expecting it to be bad news. I opened it to find a note from Fancy Finnerty and two tickets for the Royal Dublin Horse Show. The note read

'A small thank you for the day at the races. The Ridire Chaorach, RIP, and the rest of us had a great afternoon. I'm due to have some fluid taken off my lungs, but other than that I'm soldiering on'.

Holy Mother of Jesus! How was I going to get out of sharing this with Sr. Josephine? Was I even going to try? She looked at me expectantly and held out her hand. I passed over the letter like a child. She read it, pursed her lips, nodded and handed it back without a word. As usual I wanted to babble an explanation, but I just put the note and the tickets back in the envelope and made to leave. She smiled at me. I knew from experience that when Sr. Josephine smiled it was time to be worried, very worried.

'Nothing happens on my ward Nurse without me finding out about it' she said with a certainty I did not doubt. I should also have known that I should never have underestimated her ability to discover sooner or later everything that had gone on. Trust me; I had been living on borrowed time.

'You were sold out for a bottle of stout' she said sorrowfully.

Stout was given to patients who needed building up, but in this instance was used as a bribe. I nodded in resignation waiting for her continue.

'Sr. Bernardino doesn't know she said, and I'd like to keep it that way'.

'Well, it's a good job I don't like stout then' I said with surprising cheek. I thought I heard a laugh disguised as a cough as I closed the door.

~ AUGUST ~

Chapter 32

I hadn't been due to go on night duty until September but with a backlog of culchies due to go on holidays now that harvest was over, or who were awaiting news that their locality was listed as free from infection, I had already done a month by the time it was my turn. Also by the beginning of August I had added several more Chapters of Bacteriology to my training and could now bore on ligionella, klebsiella, salmonella and pseudomonas, knew the difference between gram positive spore forming, gram positive non spore forming, and acid fast weak gram positive bacilli. Because of the Polio outbreak in Cork I knew the signs and symptoms to look for, and I also knew a lot more about cancer in its many forms.

By then I knew that cancers are classed by the cells that form them and that squamous and basal cells that normally line organs are the most common cells that run amok. Our lungs, breasts, abdominal organs, reproductive organs, prostates, and colons are some of the most common sites for cancer, with blood, bone, and brain coming in the top ten. I knew that there were several dozen forms of cancer, but from a simplistic point of view all I had to know were the names and progression common to particular types of cancers we nursed. For example, in men, the commonest cancer we dealt with was squamous cell cancer of the bronchus, a result of smoking unfiltered cigarettes. This was closely followed by cancer of the mouth and tongue, also due to smoking or chewing tobacco. Mesothelioma, a form of lung cancer, we also encountered usually in men who has spent years asphalting roads. The number one cause on the women's ward was invasive, or infiltrating, ductal cancer of the breast, and while there were other cancers of breast tissue this cancer made up about 75% of cases. Advanced cancer of female reproductive organs came second, with the men keeping pace with prostatic cancer. Stomach, recto-colon, and pancreatic cancers were commoner in the men while the abnormal proliferation of cells that make up bone marrow and blood cells known as leukaemias or lymphomas, and brain tumours called glioma affected both sexes, as did sarcoma bone cancers.

The only other thing I knew was that with Radiation as the only treatment method, once the disease has spread beyond its primary site, the outcome was only a matter of time. I knew that some cancers were more aggressive than others, and spread very quickly, while others metastasized slowly over the course of several months, or even years, depending on where the cancer originated in the body. Progression was more common than regression though some patients were fortunate enough to experience the latter escaping the scythe for months longer than expected. I have often wondered just what the scientific basis for treatment was, or whether a lot of it was, of necessity, experimental. A particularly unpleasant form of cancer was neglected rodent ulcers of the face. With early intervention the prognosis was excellent, but the patients with ulcerated suppurating tumours we admitted often had a golf ball sized gap, or bigger, around the corner of the lip. The initial carcinoma was often caused by habitually smoking a clay pipe, common to men *and* women in the Gaeltacht area's of Ireland. The women's tumours were usually dealt with at an early stage, but some of the men's were appalling, and said a lot about their isolated way of life. Rodent ulcer was a good descriptive name for these skin cancers because in the later stages it often looked as if the patients face had been gnawed by a rat. Changing dressings was not a task to look forward to. The nauseating smell was made ten times worse when intermingled with the green chlorophyll scented Wick air freshener on the afflicted patient's locker.

During my year there I often wondered why there were three Hospitals' in Dublin catering for Skin and Cancer patients. It seemed an odd combination, but on reflection skin cancers would probably initially be seen by a Dermatologist so perhaps the marriage is not as odd as it seems. I also knew that the Boards of Governors of General Hospitals aided and abetted by Consultants and Matrons did not want the expense of treating these particular patients as part of their budget. Because of the specialist nature and proscribed philanthropic antecedents of most hospitals the power to do so was in their hands.

By now I was in regular correspondence with my American pen pal in the Marine Training Centre out in in the 950sq. miles of scorching Mojave Desert in Southern California. He had sent me a photo of himself and his pride and joy, his blue and white Zephyr. I have long forgotten its horse power and cylinder capacity but at the time I knew more about that car than I did about his folks. In contrast my letters included details about my family, my training, ambitions, plans and all things that interested a Dublin teenager. He was a good looking athletic nineteen years old young man whose knowledge of geography was rudimentary. Ireland was a land of leprechauns, priests and gangsters, courtesy of Disney, Bing Crosby and James Cagney, with John Wayne and Maureen O'Hara thrown in for ballast. I learned that America was not all Hollywood glamour, or happy families on spacious streets eating home made apple pie. His battalion were a microcosm of American society and several of his letters mentioned the effects of 'desegregation' on his unit. Although this had taken place several years previously he told me whites still kept with whites, coloured with coloured. Coming from a city where the only black faces we saw were around academic establishments or on collection tins for the Propagation of the Faith, the significance of racial segregation was completely lost on me. Mervin was training in the surrounding mountains and arid plains in anticipation of deployment overseas. The Korean War being over, and the Vietnam invasion still in the future, his posting would depend on the shifting allegiances and vagaries of the Cold War, but since Eisenhower showed no enthusiasm for troop involvement in either the Suez Crisis or the Hungarian revolution that year Mervin was serving his country on his home soil. He seemed to enjoy my news because he thought my life was *quaint* so I always responded to his tissue thin blue airline paper letters.

Chapter 33

When I started on Night Duty it felt like entering another world. Sleeping arrangements during the day were quite civilized in the Home, and it was one of the few things Sr. Agnes was quite strict about. Three small rooms were provided in the attic. They had previously been part of the house's servant's quarters during its days of grandeur. Apart from a peg board and a small bedside table each room contained a bed, a Holy picture and the food notice. On the narrow corridor wall was a notice saying, 'Disturbing night staff is strictly forbidden and is a disciplinary offence'. Mary Cronin, whose place I was taking told me the rules.

'Your belongings remain downstairs in your bed space, because you only come up here to sleep on your nights on she said, followed by

'You are supposed to be in bed by 11.00am unless you're attending lectures, and you're not supposed to get up before 5.00pm'.

She then tried to explain to me the night duty meal rota. For those of you confused by the day rota I now join you. Breakfast, Dinner, Tea and Supper now became

Breakfast, at 7.00pm cornflakes, toast and marmalade *or whatever was for supper if you preferred.*

Dinner, at midnight which was pre prepared *and could be substituted for the makings of a fried breakfast in the ward kitchen.*

Tea at 3.00am became tea and toast.

Supper leftovers at 8.00am or *the ubiquitous porridge breakfast before going to bed.*

Confused? So was I, but as long as I told Mary what I wanted the food appeared.

I ate a lot of breakfasts.

Night duty staff comprised a Senior Houseman on call, a Sister, Staff Nurse, two, or sometimes three probationers, and one or two Private Nurses on the Wing. Winnie Mc Whinnie was the Staff Nurse. She had no sense of humour, but obviously her parents did. We called her Queenie behind her back. She did permanent nights, and was one of the most miserable women I have ever come across in my life. Why she was allowed to nurse terminally ill patients remains a mystery to me. She was in her early thirties and having trained at St. Finbarr's in Cork had never been employed by anybody apart from the Daughters of Charity. She was quite willowy and attractive until you looked at her discontented face and trunk like legs. She had a boyfriend, Malcolm, with whom she used to bore us. I learned from Duffy he was mythical.

Queenie and Rita Carroll covered St Peter's assorted rooms and the Private Wing, but anybody who needed nursing care in the Wing had to supply their own Private Nurse at night. Sr. Apolline and I covered both St. Elizabeth's and St. Vincent's Wards on the first floor. Queenie was on nights off so Biddy Lynch was on until 10.00pm to help Carroll medicate and settle the patients. Biddy worked days on the Wing extending her shifts to 10.00pm on Mc Whinnie's nights off. Biddy, of one of the tribes of Galway, was filling in time waiting for her sister to qualify, when they would leave for Chicago. She was a fair skinned, dark hair good looking girl, and although only two years post registration, was very competent.

Our night started at 8.00pm and finished at 8.00am. Providing care for 52 patients seems a lot, and I found the idea fairly intimidating but with about 35 of them ambulant it was manageable. Carroll only had 26 but because they were semiprivate and were, in theory, more demanding. My first duty when I came on was to read the 'Nursing Book' and sign that I had read it. I did this on both wards, with the day probationers champing at the bit until I had signed, what was the official handing over of their care. To maintain harmony, the day staff came on at 7.50 am to sign the books for us, so we reciprocated by coming on at 7.50pm. Sr. Apolline took a Sister to Sister report checked the controlled drugs cupboards and night shift began. I had been told by Cronin to ensure all overhead lights were dimmed by 10.00. Although Matron lived in the Wing and could not possibly see the Ward windows she was not averse to telephoning the ward to ask for the culprit's name if the lights were still on. My fellow Probationers believed her informant was C.J. from her vista across the road.

My first job should have been to collect up all the cups from the bedtime drinks round, but I found the job done, and everything washed up and put away. Helpful ambulant patients were worth their weight in gold. They took the tea and drinks trolleys around, helped incapacitated patients with their drink, or wheeled them down to the garden or the Chapel, knew what 'Nil by mouth' meant, and the importance of intake and output charts to liver or renal patients. In this day and age they would have so many health and safety rules to contend with they would have to stand by and watch a patient die of dehydration.

'Morphine' patients were settled first so I joined Sr. Apolline by the controlled drugs cupboard on St. Elizabeth's. Like urine testing, giving morphine was not the task of a moment. The day staff had sterilized the syringes and left them on a covered tray with ampoules of 60 milligrams of sterile water, mentholated spirit lamp and a sterilized spoon. Morphine came in tablet form in dosages of ¼, ½ and 1 grain. Depending on the dosage 1 grain in 60 mls would do four ¼ grain dosages in 15 mls. This was the easiest calculation to make if you had four patients to inject, but life is never that easy, and every dosage had to be accounted for, so the ¼ and ½ grain dosages also had to be made up. Maths had never been one of my strong points but I had now got used to converting from imperial to metric and vica versa and could even calculate how many drops a minute was needed to empty a litre IV drip in eight hours. We did the same round on the men's ward. Morphine injections were given p.r.n or pro re nata which literally means 'in the circumstances' but which we interpreted as 'when needed'. Finished by 9.00pm we started the night sedation round. Everybody was written up for sedation, but surprisingly few accepted it, refusing with 'we'll see how it goes Nurse'. Bed patients and Helps were made comfortable for the night and by 10.00pm the overhead lights were dimmed and most of the patients angle poise lamps were switched off. Sr. Apolline made for her office on St. Elizabeth ward to catch up on paperwork leaving me sitting at the landing table between both wards whose doors were left wide open so that I could hear a call from any bed. Placing my cardigan over the back of the chair and my torch on the table I read through the Nursing Reports again to make sure I had forgotten nothing. I knew it was pointless putting on my cardigan until the patients settled down because I would have to remove it if one of them called out.

Chapter 34

What I had never realized is that patients had a life at night. I had always assumed that they went to bed when I went off duty, slept all night and were woken at 7.30am for breakfast. How wrong I was. The ambulant women gathered around a bed bound patient or two, and updated them on the happenings of the day, the progress of their treatment, family news, and saying a communal rosary before going to their beds when the lights were dimmed. They put pipe cleaners or rollers in each other's hair to look glamorous for Mr Riordan our Consultant Medical Director, and Dr. Courtney our Skin Specialist. The Skin's socialised more jovially in the smaller rooms, making plans for their discharge and promising to keep in touch. They partially closed the door of their rooms so that they could go on talking if they wanted to, but when I'd check them at 11.00pm they would all be fast asleep.

I still had to get to know the men on St. Vincent's Ward. I knew that the two 'Beds' had perineal tubes draining ascites fluid formed by terminal damage to the liver, and that there were three 'Helps' and the two for theatre who had 'Nil by Mouth' notices dangling from their angle poise lamps. The 'Ambulants', who had been sitting at the ward table playing cribbage and dominos and who were now all in their beds settling to sleep were still bodies under counterpanes to me. I had been aware of a fair haired, younger than usual Skin patient who, with another patient, had done the hot drinks round and cleared everything away, and had thought how nice it would be to nurse a young patient who was not going to die. At midnight Sr. Apolline asked if I wanted to take my dinner break, or relieve Carroll to have hers. Normally Carroll and I could have a break together, but with Mc Whinnie off we had to stagger our times. I learned from Carroll it was Sr. Apolline who should cover her but I was glad of the change. 'You go first' she said 'and you can cook mine at the same time'.

We had both opted for a 'cook your own breakfast fry up' instead of a reheated yesterday's day staff dinner. 'And for God's sake close the kitchen door or the smell of bacon will wake half the ward' she added. Having followed her instructions I had two plates of food, bread buttered and tea made and on the table in no time at all. She came in, opened the window to dispel the smell, put on a kettle to boil, and we sat at the table, leaving the door open, and instead of staggering our breaks gobbled everything down with our usual speed. 'What's the kettle for I asked'? Looking at her fob watch she raised a finger and said 'Give it a minute'. The kettle was just about to boil when there was a cough and a whispered 'Nurse' from St Peter's room.' Is there any tea going'?

Sr. Apolline disappeared into her office on St. Elizabeth's on my return. In theory she was to be responsive to any patient who called out, and to be available to offer me and Carroll advice and guidance. However neither of us dared disturb her unless it was to give morphine. We knew she had a duty to say her 'Office' which was a list of prescribed prayers, but I suspected she indulged in a nice little doze as well. She would reappear at 3.00am to allow me a tea break which I again took with Carroll, and she would again ensconce herself in her office this time until 5.00am when I had be in the ward kitchens buttering bread for the patient's breakfast. Having completed that task I would put the porridge on in double boilers, go to the sluice room to boil the syringes and get ready for the start of the day at 6.00am. While the overhead lights didn't get turned up until 7.00am, sunrise, at 5.30am made it kind of redundant. The same two ambulant patient's did the early morning tea round for me, the young one cheerfully telling me that he had saved me a trip to Matron by adding water to a boiled dry double boiler. This sent me dashing to St. Elizabeth's to find that that one too was also being saved by the tea trolley brigade. The ward maids came on at 7.00am, and much to my relief breakfast then became their responsibility. Between 6.00am and 7.50am I had a list of nursing duties to complete, and the Nursing Book to write up before the day staff appeared. The two patients for theatre would be having radium rods inserted in their tongues, so apart from keeping them fasting there was little or no preparation apart from putting a theatre pack beside each bed.

I had been cruising on adrenaline all night but as soon as my head hit the pillow at 9.00am I went out like a light. I woke refreshed and ready to go again. Looking at my watch it said 6.00pm. It was time to get up. I made my way to the bathroom to find Mary cleaning it.

'You should be in your bed by now Nurse' she said 'but if you want to wait I only have to sluice the floor'.

There was something about her sentence that didn't make sense, but it was the smell of dinner wafting up the stairs that permeated my brain.

'What time is it I asked her'?

'It's about half eleven' she told me.

Jezzis wept! I had read the time upside down and had only been asleep for two and a half hours. I went back to bed and lay there with my eyes boring holes in the ceiling. Being under the eves the room was hot in summer, and allegedly freezing in winter. I had the window open because of the stuffiness and suddenly became acutely aware of the noise.

'*Where had all these bloody birds come from*'?

The wood pigeons with their hollow coos sang in duet with the three syllable coos of their cousins, the collared doves. Blackbirds and song thrushes gave piercing choral support, while the house sparrows and tits chirruped and twittered on the sidelines. Apart from me, the only dissent seemed to come from quarrelsome starlings perched on a telephone wire. I tossed and turned for hours until I pulled up the blind and decided to try reading a text book. Without turning a page I was dead to the world. When Mary gave me the 6.00pm call I wished I could just roll over and sleep for the night.

Chapter 35

We started off the night with Mc Whinnie and Carroll on duty downstairs. Myself and Sr..Apolline were upstairs with Sr. Vincent's 'Specialling' the two post op patients until 10.00pm. This was not the first time I would nurse patients with radium rods embedded in the tongue but it would be the first time at night. The first twenty four hours were the most critical because of the tongue swelling up and blocking the upper airway. Lying sedated on drips and oxygen in neighbouring beds both patients had an emergency tracheotomy tray on their bedside lockers with a suction machine being shared. Sedation was a mixed blessing. It made life easier for the patient but cloaked early signs of obstruction. The main reason for the sedation was to prevent patients pulling out any of the half inch radium rods sewn into the tongue. Each rod had a top like a threaded needle which had a long black thread attached to it. They had to be checked frequently to ensure the rods were still in situ. There would be no prayer reading over departing souls here. This was a full on resuscitation situation and I knew that when Sr. Vincent went off at 10.00pm at some point they were going to become my responsibility. Before she went off I asked her to go through the emergency procedure with me. I had mixed feelings about asking Sr. Apolline anything. She was not unpleasant, or prone to rages like Sr. Bernardino, but she had no interest in helping Probationers learn, or acquire new skills, and although she never said it you felt that on the tip of her tongue was the words 'look it up'. The patients too found her unapproachable and lacking in empathy. One of the women put it very succinctly

'When she looks at me I can feel her willing me to lie quietly and keep my counterpane straight'.

'I think most of the danger of any further swelling is probably over Nurse' Sr. Vincent said yawning after a long day. 'But just in case, they are to be closely observed until they are seen by Mr. Riordan in the morning, so we'll go through the procedure'.

'If either of the patients show any signs of difficulty breathing tell Sr. Apolline, and ask her if you should phone the Houseman and let him know'.

'If the patient stops breathing then you only have three minutes to save his life, and I do mean you' she said looking at me seriously.

Holy Mary mother of God!

'Then follow these instructions' she said handing me a sheet of paper.

'Read them through' she advised. 'Sr. Apolline will take over until midnight'.

Once the lights were dimmed I read the instructions

<u>EMERGENCY TRACHEOTOMY; 3 MINUTES</u>

Pull the bed away from the wall
Remove head of bed and pillows
Fold pillow and place under patient's neck
Extend neck.
Open pack and attach scalpel to handle
Find thyroid cartilage (Adams apple)
Move finger down an inch until you feel cricoid cartilage
<u>*The indentation between the two is the cricoid membrane*</u>
<u>*where the incision will be made*</u>
Make a firm half inch horizontal incision about a ½ inch deep
There may be a little bleeding but place your finger inside the slit to open it
Insert the tube in the incision roughly 1' deep and secure tapes around neck

Apply suction to tube quickly. Remove oxygen mask from oxygen tube and apply tube intermittently to tracheotomy tube. Patient should then be able to breathe unaided.

Place oxygen mask over tracheotomy to improve patient's oxygen uptake.

In the event that the patient does not respond to suction and oxygen; breathe into the tube with two quick breaths. Pause for five seconds, and then give one breath every five seconds.

You will see the chest rise and the person should regain consciousness if you have performed the procedure correctly the patient should be able to breathe on their own.

Remembering my fiasco with Paddy Joe Delaney there would be no mistake this time. When I took over at midnight I watched them like a hawk recording respiration, pulse and colour every quarter of an hour. I had no compunction about poking them periodically to make sure they were revivable; neither of them was going to die on *my* watch. The night flew. I saw nothing of Carroll, opting to take my breaks on the Ward, without a word of appreciation from Sr. Apolline who still went to her Office over on Elizabeth Ward as usual. For the first time I was acutely aware of the sounds of a ward at night, identifying coughs, sighs, groans, creaks and rustles from various beds. Come dawn one of my tea trolley brigade rose to get the early morning drinks ready, and finding I hadn't had the opportunity to butter the bread or put the porridge on, did it for me. When Sr. Apolline came out of her office to start the Morphine round I pointed out to her that I had not got anything done over on Elizabeth Ward because I had been unable to leave St. Vincent's Ward. She looked at me as if I was I was half witted.

'Those patients don't need 'Specialling' at this stage Nurse' she said 'so get on with your work'.

I knew little about Sr. Apolline, but even allowing for my inexperience, I had absolutely no confidence in her judgement because I believed it was based on making life easier for herself and not on patient comfort or welfare. I also had the fear that if anything happened I would be left carrying the can.

'Let me just record that in the Nursing Book, Sister' I said opening the book.

I got no further.

A disgruntled Rita Carroll was sent up to cover Elizabeth Ward while an equally disgruntled Mc Whinnie had to do her own menial tasks downstairs. With the ward now awake and my young skin patient doling out urinals and gathering up tea cups I got everything done by 07.20 and handed over two drowsy but alive post operative patients. I went into the Skin rooms to find my helper. Scrutinising all ten patients I couldn't find him. Like the Scarlet Pimpernel he had vanished into thin air.

Chapter 36

I slept for a solid nine hours and went back duty determined to seek out the elusive Pimpernel. Collaring him washing up in the kitchen I interrogated him. Apart from telling me his name, and that he was a private patient going out of his mind with boredom over on the Wing, I learned little else. I had no intention of dissuading him from helping and socializing with the men so I let him get on with it. My two post ops were awake but doped with pain relief. They were both feeling miserable, existing on chipped ice and intravenous fluids. They were also on enforced bed rest in case a rod got lost. Having difficulty swallowing they had towels around their necks to absorb the constant dribble, but despite all this discomfort one of them asked me for a cigarette. I couldn't wait to get them sedated for the night. The tracheotomy trays were still on the locker tops but I had lost my dread of them, and to reassure me, observations had been dropped to half hourly. It was several years before I learned that I had been exposed to unacceptable doses of radiation at St. Anne's. We were not issued with Radiation Detection badges although they were available at the time.

Over the next week I grew to love night duty. I slept very well and enjoyed a deepening relationship with the patients. There was time to talk to them at their most vulnerable, and to write letters home for those with little schooling. The worst hour of the night was between 4.00 and 5.00am. Sitting on the landing wrapped in a cardigan, and with nobody awake, a kind of paralysis creeps over your body as if you had been injected with curare. Your hearing becomes so acute you could hear a pin drop and you feel as if you have turned into the living dead, and will only move again using super human will power. You wait for somebody to call 'Nurse' to see if you can reactivate movement. So far I had always managed to get to my feet, though it took several steps to get the circulation working, and several more seconds to regain the power of speech.

Jarvis Vincente, the Scarlet Pimpernel, was full of surprises. He was neat and compact and bore some resemblance to Alan Ladd. He was twenty eight and English born was being treated for stress related psoriasis and was a Religious Brother attached to a Congregation of Priests. Most of our culchie patients had no interest in the English soccer scene, but on introducing them to the intricate rules of the 'Littlewoods Treble Draw' Jarvis had them hooked. The cribbage, domino and playing cards were cleared from the central table in St. Vincent's as the sports section of papers were perused before making a selection. All I knew was that your chances of winning were related to the number of games drawn and the number of home and away wins forecast by filling in a form. There was no radio on the ward so come Saturday tea time there was nothing for it but to wait for the late edition of the Herald or Mail to appear. Winning was a pipe dream, what they enjoyed most was their skill at forecasting. For the cancer patients it was a great diversion, something to take their minds off treatment and outcomes. Henry O'Keefe, feeling miserable after several bouts of radium asked me to fill in his form. What I knew about football teams was pitiful, but having listened to the results on the radio late Saturday afternoons for years I at least knew some of the teams likely to draw. I filled the form with a mixture of possible draws and scores and forgot all about it. The excitement when I went on duty on Saturday night was electric. Henry had won £48. I was delighted for him, but soon regretted my part in his win when I had to endure the resultant pleas for my winning formula from the rest of the syndicate, plus a lecture from Sr. Apolline on the unseemliness of my behaviour. However I did wonder if the curse had been lifted. I didn't have to wait long to find out.

Just before the day staff went off there had been a death on the Wing. Queenie had laid the woman out and now wanted help removing her to the mortuary, more familiarly known as the Room of Repose behind the Chapel. She was a Hungarian-Viennese woman whom we called Mrs. Von for short her double-barrelled name which sounded like 'Gesundheit' being too much of a mouthful for everyday use. She had spent a few days in St. Ann's Ward some months previously where, speaking very little English, she has still managed to complain incessantly any time a window was opened.

'Oy, Oy, mine Gott, oy vey iz mir, the vind, the vind, I vill die' she would wail as fresh air wafted in during bed making.

I had helped Mc Whinnie put her on the trolley and covered her shrouded body with the raised purple velvet canopy. At this point another patient's bell rang and Mc Whinnie disappeared.

Knowing that Sr. Apolline was quite capable of going off for her break without checking that I was back on the ward I decided that I could manage the trolley myself the short distance across the pathway from the nearby side door to the mortuary. Seventy or so yards, clear run, no steps or corners. Checking that the key to the mortuary was on the trolley I gave it an initial push and was on my way. I must have managed a good fifty yards before an unexpected fierce gust of wind caught the canopy lifting it into the air and spinning it across the garden. Taking me by surprise the trolley veered sideways leaving three wheels on the pathway and the forth sinking into the grass verge. In trying to right it the wheel parted company with the trolley and Mrs. Von, in early rigor, took on a new lease of life as she moved smoothly towards the tilt. The rest of the path to the mortuary door was like a mad dance of the macabre with me trying to raise the wheel-less corner while clutching Mrs. Von under the chin to stop her sliding off as I manoeuvred the trolley along. Reaching the mortuary door I realised that the key was no longer on the trolley. It was at this point that the heavens opened and I was aware that I was being observed. The two eye pennies had got lost in the struggle. The hooded eyed sardonic glance from the drenched corpse didn't have to tell me I was cursed. I knew.

Oye, Oye, mine Gott, the vind, the vind and the rain…oy vey iz mir!

On the last of my nine nights on I realised that Jarvis would probably be discharged by the time I returned to duty, and that like the patients on St. Vincent's Ward I would miss him. He had told me his religious Order was sending him on an enclosed Retreat to give him time to consider whether he had taken the right path in life. Although he was twenty eight I felt he had missed out on being young and carefree, and that he loved his motor bike as much as God. He treated Rita and I to breakfast in the Copper Kettle in Leeson St. on our last morning, he then roaring off on his Norton while I staggered off to bed to get a few hours sleep before heading off for a night at Grans so that we could have an early start the following morning. Yes, God help me, the day of shopping for wedding finery was upon us. I had made it plain to the Gran that this was a one off expedition. The following day Bina Corcoran and I were off to the Royal Dublin Horse Show in Ballsbridge with the tickets Fancy Finnerty had sent me, and the day after I had to get some hour's kip before returning to duty at 8.00pm.

I'm sure you're all waiting with bated breath for all the lurid details, and have such little faith in my tolerance that you consider what I tell you will have been exaggerated beyond reason. Well, all I can say to those of you of such little faith is that you have never shopped with Granny Redmond.

Chapter 37

With a full Irish breakfast inside me, and the sun slanting across the Dwellings, Tess, the Gran and I were waiting for Sheila and her two children to arrive. The latter age twelve and ten were young enough to get away with their belligerent expressions and bolshi attitudes, I was not. I assumed they had now been told the news and as I had foreseen were not 'sick with excitement'. Tess and Sheila had already reccied the shops so had a good idea what was available. However they were not on the same page of the hymn book. Sheila had had a utilitarian wedding at the height of the Emergency with clothes rationing at its most stringent, so Tess was going to have the fairytale wedding *she* would have loved. Tess wanted a dress like Princess Grace, but otherwise had no fixed opinions. Gran on the other hand had very fixed opinions. Her plan was to hold out for the best price, therefore we must choose a shop that could kit us *all* out to capitalise on the most discount.

Although Dublin is a fair sized City it was not commercially cosmopolitan or renowned for its designers in the 1950's so Bridal Shops were uncommon. A specialist section in Department Stores, or having dresses made by a personal dress maker was the norm, so I tried to extol the talents of May Grant again. In vain; we set off for town down the local backstreets into North Earl Street. Several shops and three hours later we stopped for dinner in Woolworths in Henry St. where Eamón and Carol were cheered up with jelly and ice cream. Every shop we had gone into had the same range of dresses in the same pastel shades as a box of Willwoods Fondant Crèmes. What none of them stocked was a full length bridesmaid dress to fit a 5'1" size 12, or a white satin suit to fit a twelve year old. All bridesmaids' dresses, no matter what the colour, were intended for well nourished 5'4"s or taller and little boys over the age of six didn't wear white satin suits. Any sensible person reading this would think 'buy the chosen wedding dress and the lemon sherbet flower girls dress and let May do the rest', but I was not with sensible people. The Gran conceded the satin suit was a lost cause, but there was still a chance of rigging me out, so back we went to Boyers who were holding on to a wedding and a flower girls dress, as were two other shops. We now went through the ballerina length dresses for bridesmaids, and lo and behold there were three in my size, pink candyfloss, luminous lime green or glorious orangey peach. However the only one with a matching head dress was the candyfloss pink, so the choice was easy.

Sheila, the kids and I abandoned the expedition at this point leaving Tess, and the Gran, cash secreted in her liberty bodice, to retrace their steps to see which floor walker would do the best deal.

'Thank God, that's over' I said heaving a sigh of relief. Sheila looked at me with pity.

'You've obviously forgotten the shoes' she said. 'And you'll have to cut that hair' she said with a critical glance at my coiled tresses. 'You'll never get that head of hair under that little cloche cap.

The thought of a shoe shopping traipse was deeply depressing and I said so. Having a size 3 foot and a high instep meant a limited choice so I vowed to find the shoes before involving Gran.

'So, does that mean you don't want to help me find a rigout to wear' Sheila said in her 'after all I've done for you voice'.

Too bloody true, there wasn't a Plenary Indulgence big enough to tempt me. I might get no remission in Purgatory or improve my

Karma but at least I'd escape hell on earth if she and I went shopping without the Gran. I was still getting fallout about the coat. Anyway that could wait until my next days off. For now I was going to enjoy my day at the Royal Dublin Horse Show.

Fancy's tickets were for the Stands where the hoi poli would be congregating so dressed in a combination of everybody's finery Corcoran and I set of for Ballsbridge. While commercial Dublin might be regarded as provincial, the same could not be said about this gathering as we rubbed shoulders with Foreign Royalty, International Diplomats, West Britain's and home grown bourgeoisie in the form of horse breeders and moneyed farmers. We were lead to our seats which were in a covered stand, thank God, because the sun was already beating down, and between Bina's red hair and my own melanin deficient shin we would have burned to a crisp in the unsheltered areas. The usher who had escorted us to our seats had handed us passes to the stabling yard where we could go and see the horses being paraded and examined before the jumping events. The main event of the day was the Aga Khan Cup so we watched the five teams parading around the course before the lunch interval. Note, no mid day *dinner* here, these were people who *lunched*. But in fact it was going to be no food at all for us; the prices knocked us off our feet. Returning to our seats with a packet of Rowntrees Pastilles, and having slaked our thirst at the horses water tap in the Yard I found a note on my seat which read 'Please come to Stand Entrance B and find me', signed, Usher'. Knowing I was cursed, a furious Corcoran said

'I bet somebody has complained about us drinking the horse's water'.

In some trepidation we headed for the usher, who, on seeing us was grovelling with apologies. When he had given us our passes he should also have given us 'these'. 'These' turned out to be two coupons for the Refreshment Tent. We heaped blessings on Fancy, his ancestors and his progeny as we filled our stomachs and then watched Great Britain, Ireland, Italy, Spain, and USA battle it out in the main Arena. The main disappointment of the day was not seeing anything of Fancy the other was when we discovered the Aga Khan was not in attendance to award the Italian Team Captain, Piero D'Inzeo, the cup. It was going to be presented by President DeValera, or as my Granda used to refer to him 'The Cute Hoor'. During one of my childhood holidays in Claregalway I had gone to the funeral of the local Canon, a renowned bully, whose death I allegedly caused. Even then I was cursed! The funeral was a grand affair and was attended by DeValera, the Taoiseach at the time. When I mentioned the latter to Granda Redmond his, not unexpected, but disgusted response was 'did nobody think to bring a gun with them'?

Chapter 38

Returning to another nine nights of night duty I found Sr. Apolline was back on days and I was now on with Sr. Vincent. The difference was unbelievable. Sr. Vincent had the look of somebody who never went out in the sun. Her pallor was in no way enhanced by the seagull headpiece or the starched white apparel that acted as a collar and bib at the same time. She had a sturdy farmers daughters frame, and had, as match makers would say 'great childbearing hips'. She was a good ward sister, with a calmness and kindness that belied her efficiency and was considerate to her staff. On day duty she always tried to make sure her Probationers had their weekly study time even if it meant her rolling up her sleeves and getting stuck in to whatever needed doing. I now discovered that I was not going to cruise through night duty without assessment or study. While Sr. Apolline's attitude had been of the 'Don't ask me, look it up' variety Sr. Vincent's was 'If you don't know, ask me'. The latter proved to be a two way street because I never knew when she would decide to quiz me out of the blue, so my brain was going to have to come out of hibernation.

Having got used to Sr. Apolline ensconsing herself in her office for hours on end, it was a shock to the system to find Sr. Vincent joining me on the landing.' I'll get that' she'd say making her way to a patient who'd called out. Her keenness was making me redundant so I took to pacing the wards flashing my torch on patients in the hope they would wake up and want something. I would even have taken on the worry of 'Specialling' but there were no post ops and the 'Beds' were happily sedated. After a few nights, Carroll, who was on her last rota and would be returning to days got fed up with me moaning.

'Christ Almighty Redmond I'll swap with you' the usually quiet Carroll shouted in exasperation, 'A night with Queenie and you'd soon appreciate what you've got' she went on, slapping me across the back with a damp tea towel.

Too true; I decided to tell Sr. Vincent how I felt.

'I thought you would like a bit of time to read' she told me.

When I assured her that my brain wasn't constructed to acquire knowledge in the early hours of the morning she understood.

'I know Nurse, I have the same difficulty keeping my mind on my 'Office'' she confessed. 'I only hope God forgives my lack of enthusiasm.

We compromised on our response to patients, she would do St. Elizabeth's, and I would do St. Vincent's.

Several nights later we came on duty to find Murty Neary moribund and being 'Specialled' by Sr. Catherine. Murty was one of our patients with a horrendous rodent ulcer that had eaten away most of his right cheek. He had had a massive cerebral haemorrhage during the day and had been given the Last Rites. His brother and sister in law were on their way from Mayo so we had a problem. Should we disturb him while he was peacefully slipping away to make him presentable, or if he died could we disrespectfully disturb the transit of his soul to lay him out? Sr. Vincent went for a modified version of the former so we had to start by concentrating on the smell. The smell of putrefying flesh has a gagging effect unless you put a dab of Vicks Vapour Rub under your nose. The Wicks chlorophyll air freshener cum smell masker used by the Hospital made me as sick as the purification. It was decided to move Murty to the far corner of the windowed side of the ward once we had redressed his face and removed the naso-gastric tube that had been used to nourish him. Replacing the dressing involved removing the present pack which involved a large piece of gamgee big enough not to fall into the cavity. The new pack was covered with a piece of oil skin to keep any exudate from seeping through, and the whole lot was wrapped in a crepe bandage around the head. The plan was to open the nearest window and sprinkle the bandage with 4711 eau de Cologne when the family arrived. Sr. Vincent had me bring in every vase of flowers from the cool of St. Elizabeth's sluice room and put them on the central table. To make sure there was no residual smell I had to scrub down Murty's original bed space and replace the curtains.

Shortly after the lights were dimmed for the night the family arrived. They found Murty reeking of lavender, a ward full of flowers and a candle lit locker top set ready for saying the prayers for the dying. Most of the ward was still awake, the medicine round having fallen by the way side. Sr. Vincent encouraged a couple of Ambulants to do another hot drinks round. 'All we need is a drop of medicinal brandy and we have the makings of a wake' a wag commented. Sister gazed at him reproachfully but I noticed an empty bottle of medicinal brandy in the Dispensary crate later. Coming up to midnight Murty was fading away so we gathered around the bed to say the Prayers for the Dying. Sister lit the candles and pulled the curtain back from the foot of the bed to allow anybody still awake to participate. Although the side curtains sheltered Murty from sight, and all the patients saw were shadows from the glow of the candles I had mixed feeling about terminally ill patients witnessing death, but if truth be told they seemed to appreciate it. I think there was a mixture of vicarious delight that it wasn't their turn, and a reassurance that death would be peaceful and respectful. On her way to bed Sr.

Catherine took the family over to the Wing to find them a room for the night. When Sr. Vincent and I were laying Murthy out later I made some very judgemental remarks about the family allowing him to get into such a state before seeking medical aid.
'Only God can judge people Nurse, so unless He has designated you His mouthpiece you should keep your opinions to yourself' she told me firmly. I blushed with embarrassment. She was right of course; I knew nothing of the family circumstances.

~ SEPTEMBER ~

Chapter 38

The eleventh of September dawned bright and crisp with a sky full of fluffy cirrus clouds that boded well for the day. Before the smell of breakfast drifted in to the bedroom the sound of church bells and seagulls told me I was home in the Dwellings. Tess was already up and having her hair put into curlers by Irene Fitz. The wedding wasn't until eleven so with three hours to kill I donned my pink satin dressing gown and sat down to breakfast. I had reached such a state of resignation that I even considered praying for redemption or at least for the curse to be lifted, if only for the day. Bereft of my tresses there would be no hair styling for me. I now had a sleek short bob. Correction; I now had my hair cut in what should have been a sleek short bob, but my hair developed a mind of its own curling in three different directions. This was already giving me grief at the hospital. Walking past Matron, who happened to be having time off from her *'Custody of the Eyes'* she told me curtly

'Off the face Nurse' looking at my hair flopping around my forehead.

Hair lacquer and hairgrips were about to become the order of the day. God only knows what I was going to do when it had grown half way down my neck.

I had come home the night before for Tess's equivalent of a 'Girls Night Out'. In days when respectable women didn't go in to Pubs unless they were old enough to be drawing a pension, or were willing to confine themselves discretely to the snug, this was in fact a 'Women's Night In' and involved the four flats on the landing opening their front doors for common usage as they had on the day of Granda's death. With about twenty invited guests and an expected two dozen, who 'would just call by' this co-operation was necessary for any big social occasion. The occasion itself cost little. Assorted sandwiches, biscuits and cake were provided by Gran in No. 31. For grandeur her Art Deco plates were being used, with a doily on each serving plate, and paper napkins to catch the crumbs as everybody helped themselves. This all emphasised the specialness of the occasion. Annie in No.32 moved her kitchen chairs into the communal hall for extra seating, provided cups of tea, replenished the sandwiches and provided a cloakroom for those hardy enough to remove their coats. Annie was also the keeper of the wedding frocks which were under lock and key in her camphor soaked wardrobe. Madge Kelly, in No.30 protected her mahogany table with green baize, newspaper and a table cloth, then set out glasses for minerals and the Trinity; Power's, Port and Porter. Marion Farrell, in No.29, the only one with young children took them, and her husband, round to her Ma on the back terrace so that she could enjoy herself. The guests would turn up with a supply of drink, and wedding presents which were put under Tess's bed and would not be opened until after the wedding. Before anybody got down to enjoying the evening, finery for those attending the wedding, was swapped and borrowed to defray the cost. Sarah Breslin loaned me the family pearls which had belonged to her deceased niece Bridget. She had died tragically five years previously and they were out of the Pawn for the occasion. A lot of bawdy talk and a prolonged sing-along petered out coinciding with the last dregs of the Port and Annie's clock striking eleven. Marion Farrell and Madge went on hosting the party until it died on its feet but I had already drifted off to the anaesthetising effects of stale porter and the strains of 'Irene Goodnight' being sung by a maudlin Irene Fitz.

Washed, breakfasted, hair lacquered and dressed in my candyfloss pink I kept out of the way while Tess was primped, crimped and adorned by several turbaned acolytes. I looked at the vision in pink in Annie's wardrobe mirror. Apart from smelling of mothballs and a hint of Jeyes Fluid ineptly disguised by 'Evening in Paris' I looked okay from my neat little head dress down to my pink strappy sandals. Little did I realise it was the footwear that was to to be the curse the day.

I had managed to get out of a shoe shopping fest with the Gran by whizzing around and finding the shoes myself. It took three such sessions to realise that size 3 pink shoes did not exist, so I was ecstatic with relief when I found pink strappy court heeled sandals. Not only found them, but found them in a sale, and they were so comfortable it was like floating on air. I put a deposit on them and told Tess. All of you will by now expect me to exaggerate the outcome, that is, apart from the few who knew Granny Redmond's obsession with bargain hunting. I'm sure that to this day she has St. Peter scourged trying to get a better deal on her mansion above.

On my next visit home the shoe box was presented to me.

Opening it I found a pair of white sandals identical to the ones I had put a deposit on. I looked at a tight lipped Tess who said nothing.

'I thought they had to be pink' I said in outraged tones, remembering my trek to every bloody shoe shop in Dublin.

It transpired that Gran had gone to 'pick up the sandals'. No, I'll start that sentence again. It transpired that when the Gran had gone to beat the price of the sandals down further she discovered the white pair was half the price.

'You were paying good money for a pot of dye' she said with a finality that tolerated no argument.

I personally didn't care what colour shoes I was going to wear but in Tess and Sheila's scheme of things I was wearing a ballerina length pink dress ergo my shoes would be seen, ergo they should be pink. The reason for Tess's tight lip expression became evident when it was discovered that the Paddy Lynch the local cobbler did not have much demand for dyeing sandals pink. Navy, tan, brown and black were on offer. I took the sandals back to the Nurses home with me to see if a more upmarket cobbler could oblige. Red and blue only were added to the range so I decided to try an experiment. I added cochineal to white shoe cleaning paste. The outcome was a disaster.

The leather turned a blotchy pink while the stitching turned a permanent shade of fuchsia. Failing to remove all traces of the concoction, and with the wedding fast approaching, I no longer had the option of white sandals. Sharing this tale of woe in the sitting room Bina Corcoran came up with the brilliant idea of transforming the now sad specimens with a coat of nail varnish. Make up bags were raided until a suitable shade of pink was found. Sufficient was bought before I went to bed the following morning, and that day I slept in a roomful of acetate fumes having applied the Damask Rose varnish to the shoes.

The result was gratifying. I now had glossy pink shoes, colour co-ordinated, and fit to grace any wedding.

Chapter 39

Our Lady of Lourdes Church in Lower Gloucester Street was the given name of the local parish church, but to locals it was the Tin Chapel near the Monto, or the Gloucester Diamond, depending on whether their knowledge of the area was based on pursuing prostitutes or frequenting pubs. It was designated as the Chapel of Ease for the Pro Cathedral in nearby Marlborough Street. Concrete and tin on the outside, the interior was wall to wall and floor to ceiling pine. The orangey gloss of the pine gave everyone an unhealthy jaundiced hue on a fine day, but provided a warm glow at evening services.

Jennings limos were used for funerals and weddings alike. At weddings they sported white satin ribbons from silver bonnet mascot to side mirrors and the driver wore grey as opposed to funeral black. Gran and Annie Lawlor had already been taken to the church leaving plenty of time for my Da, Tess and I to make it down the stairs and out to the pavement. Being Tuesday there were only preschool kids in the grush as my father threw coppers and sweets in the air for them. Everybody in the Dwellings came out to line the pavement as Tess appeared. She looked absolutely stunning, every inch a princess with a lovely cascading bouquet of dark red roses. Most of the neighbours were going to the Wedding Service, and having done their oohing and aahing, would be taking the short cut down Bella Street and across the Bunkey Hill to the Tin Chapel. To give them the chance to get there before us we did a few small detours at a funereal pace, well practiced by the driver, arriving at the appointed time.

Sheila was in the Church doorway with Eamón and Carol. Eamón well scrubbed and Brycreamed was hunched over in his white satin shirt and trousers hoping that if he scrunched himself up small enough nobody would notice him. Carol looked very pretty and was ribboned and curled to excess. Her lemon sherbet shepherdess dress was sweet but she too looked as if she wished she was anywhere that did not involve walking down an aisle. I noticed that she had been allowed white shoes which made me aware of my own feet which were beginning to ache. Off to take her seat their Mother gave them 'the Look' and me permission to kill them if they did anything to 'show her up'. With Tess on my fathers arm and the two prospective victims walking behind me we made it up the packed Church to the alter rail.

I remember very little about the Service that followed apart from the fact that my feet felt squashed in shoes that had initially fitted like a glove. From walking on air I had progressed to standing on hot coals. While the photographs were being taken I had a chance to look down at my feet and discovered weal's forming between the straps. The nail varnish had completely destroyed any give or natural stretch in the leather so my toes were encased in two vices. The agony was exquisite. How I made it to the Function Rooms in Westland Row is a mystery but the relief of being able to take my shoes off on the cold marble floor is something I will forever cherish. The care and control of my young cousins was the last thing on my mind but they survived the day so they must have behaved. I managed to speak with aged Aunts and catch up with old neighbours.

It was strange to see Annie Lawlor in a coat. She had habitually worn the local black shawl as long as I had known her but it was now threadbare so she and the Gran had gone shopping, Gran wanting anything but black, and Annie unwilling to consider any other colour on the premise that she would be attending more funerals than weddings. Annie looked very smart but quite mournful choosing violets to adorn her black straw hat. The Gran, usually a very fashionably dressed woman on special occasions, let her purse dictate her choice, and was wearing an oatmeal colour herringbone tweed coat two sizes too big and an enormous shapeless black fur hat. 'Holy Mother of God, *what does she look like*' I'd said to Annie in tones of horror. 'A sack of oats with a dead cat on top' was Annie's tart response.

I laughed so much it reminded me that I needed to empty my bladder. Carrying my shoes I went off to find the Toilets I discovered they were the 'Penny in the Slot' type and having been burdened with a bouquet all morning I had neither purse, nor 'Mad money'. I waited for somebody to come out and caught the door before it could close. Having relieved myself I sat and crinkled and crackled the shoes picking the lacquer off until they felt quite flexible again. They ended up looking as if they had a bad case of psoriasis. I couldn't bear the thought of putting them on again, firstly because of the state of my feet but also because I still had to join in the dancing.

With my mind distracted I totally forgot the yards of net in my dress so on exiting the loo I let the door close behind me trapping a good segment of skirt. I would have to wait for somebody to come in to use the facilities to release me. Eventually the groom's mother arrived. Dressed in Carmelite brown with a hat wore so low over her eyes it looked like a WW1 soldiers helmet I at first thought she hadn't seen me, or was deaf. I explained my predicament but apart from a sympathetic 'yes, yes' she completely ignored me and put her penny in one of the other doors. I vaguely remember somebody mentioning she was German so I racked my brains for something useful to say in German, but the only words that came to mind were peremptory. 'Wenn Sie nicht gehorchen schiesse ich' seemed a bit extreme while schnell, schnell might panic her. A simple' Vortreten' might get her near enough for me to grab her bag and get a penny. When she came out she smiled nervously at me and went to a sink to wash her hands. I mimed my predicament for her and held out my hand gesturing to her bag and saying simply 'I need a penny.' 'Yes, yes' she said smiling sweetly, nodding as she left the room. Now I know that I'm cursed, and that blaspheming and blaming other people does not help, but I was fuming that nobody had come looking for me. I also pondered on the fact that we might now be joined in marriage to a family of feckin morons.

Chapter 40

Back on night duty picking at slivers of wedding cake I regaled an interested Sr. Vincent with the highlights of the wedding. Needless to say I left out any details that did not portray us as a perfectly normal family. Rita Carroll was now on days on St Elizabeth Ward so I was joined on nights by Bina. This was her second time, her previous allocation having been a short one. She would be leaving the end of October and I would miss her. Patients came and went and Sr. Vincent being a good teacher I continued to gain confidence in nursing tasks and report writing. Several new Probationers had started training, making me now the forth most senior. Of the original group only Rita, Bina, and Mary Cronin were left. Rita had told me that some English hospital Matrons were in Dublin on a recruitment drive and persuaded me to accompany her to the various hotel lounges to let the Matrons give us the once over. Armed with our training Schedules we presented ourselves for interrogation and scrutiny while consuming the coffee and biscuits provided at each venue. All four Matrons we saw offered us a place 'subject to completion of our course and acceptance by the hospital's Board of Governors', the latter I knew was a mere formality if Matron had given us the nod. It was gratifying and a huge relief to realise our General training was assured. Our futures could be in Birmingham, Liverpool, London or Manchester. Both Rita and I had been very taken by Grace Laing, the Matron of a Hospital in London's East End. Sitting with her and three other possible recruits in Wynn's Hotel I felt she had a genuine interest in our individual backgrounds and reasons for emigrating. It was also reassuring to be told that she had several ex Probationers from

St. Anne's in training and that half of her trained staff was Irish, so Carroll and I both registered an interest in joining the January set. Sheila Moran tried to sell the MRI to us while Duffy, realising that neither of us met the Army minimum height requirement agreed that London was a good choice. Within weeks we learned of our acceptance with a start date for 11th January. This spurred me on to set about planning the completion of my training. I realized that this would entail a month in Sr. Bernardino's domain. My heart sank at the prospect, but since my fellow Probationers had survived then so would I. However, while I allowed for her rants and rages I could not account for the unexplained vitriolic dislike she had of me.

September rolled to an end with all Probationers' and patients from Cork in the doldrums. They had been insufferable for weeks, bursting with bravado knowing that their Football and Hurling County Teams had made it to the All Ireland GAA Finals. On the 23rd they lost to Wexford in the hurling having already lost to Galway in the football a couple of weeks before much to the delight of my cousins and friends who had come up from Claregalway for the match. We had had no more deaths on the Wards, but several letters and Memorial cards from families of patients I had nursed in the previous months brought expected sad news. The well scrubbed Ger Reilly was one of those who had died.

The other sad news was that Sr. Catherine was leaving to transfer to the Crumlin Convent in anticipation of the opening of Our Lady's Children's Hospital in November. Although I saw little of her while I was on night duty apart from handover time I had grown very fond of her. She had taken over the day shift on St. Vincent's, and with the support of Dolly Mc Gee, a well seasoned Staff Nurse from Croom Co. Cork, had blossomed into a good ward manager. I would liked to have hugged her the morning she said goodbye, but its hard to hug somebody encased in so much starch and enveloped in so much habit, so we just held hands and I tried to hide a lump in my throat as I joked that I still hadn't forgiven her for trapping poor Rene Mc Grath in the bed the day of the enema. We were both laughing in an unseemly way when who should glide into the Ward but Sr. Bernardino. Glaring at both of us she went into the Ward office without the courtesy of telling Sr. Catherine why she was there. I knew she would never have tried that on with the other sisters, or staff nurses for that matter, and I recognised it as one of her bullying tactics. 'I've got a month with her in November' I said with resignation. 'Well you'll just have to offer it up like the rest of us' she said giving me a pat on the shoulder. 'If I can do it without whinging I'd never have to go to Purgatory' I said knowing that would not be possible.

'Well, here's a bit of advice for free' she told me seriously 'Always try to be one step ahead of her, work consciously, stand your ground and *don't* hand over your Schedule of Training to her'.

The latter advice shook me because Sr. Bernardino would be responsible for signing off my competencies and my progress report.

How do I deal with that' I asked.

'Ask for either Sr. Josephine or Sr. Vincent to be present when she does the report and get Duffy to check your competencies before you are assessed, that way she has very little power over you. 'And when it comes to it, it's only a month" she said to lighten the moment, 'You don't have to live with her'.

'In comparison, Poverty, Chastity and Obedience are the easy bits' she whispered mournfully.

Sr. Catherine must have said something about my concerns to Sr. Vincent because that night after our dinner break she came up the stairs with a green draping towel covered tray. She opened back the folds to expose a tray of gleaming steel ware. I half expected an 'Abra Ka Dabra but what I got was a factual explanation 'This, Nurse, is a General Set of surgical instruments and contains the basic requirements for most operations' she said. 'First of all you need to learn the position of every instrument, then the name, and finally the function. 'Now I've forgotten most of this so we'd better do a bit of reading up' she said producing an illustrated textbook of Surgical Nursing. Every night we went through the permutations of instruments required for the operations performed at St. Anne's with Sr. Vincent producing the instruments and me setting them out on the landing table in a prescribed manner. There must have been 50 or more but over the next few weeks I mastered them and learned the difference between Babcock and Littlewood forceps, Balfour and Weitlaner retractors, Parker and Moynihan clamps, Mayo and Kocher scissors, eight different types of clips plus dissolvable and non dissolvable stitching material. Being left handed I wondered how surgeons who were Ciotóg fared since most instruments seemed to be designed for right handed users. By November I could select any set required for the operation list of the day, so Sr. Bernardino, eat your heart out.

~ OCTOBER ~

Chapter 41

On the ward for my last nine nights in the leaf stripping month of October a teenage boy with testicular cancer, which had already metastasised into sacrococcygeal tumours had been admitted. Aidan was a Dubliner and at 18 years was a totally obnoxious pimply teenager with a brain bereft of reasoning and logic. He was thin and gangly and hadn't yet grown into his features or limbs. He was also morose, insufferable, and demanding and had been rude to staff and patients alike. Admitted for a course of Radium treatment, and living nearby in a nice salubrious neighbourhood, he was a suitable candidate for outpatient treatment.

'Why is he in here' was my first question on handover from the day staff. 'Family can't cope' was the short answer.

A fuller explanation was forthcoming from Sr. Vincent as we completed the Medicine Round.

'The parents are dead, he has two sisters a decade or so older than him who both have Civil Service careers, he has made two half hearted attempts at suicide knowing they would be home in time to find him and has threatened to do it again. They are at their wits end so he is in here until some psychiatric help can be arranged.'

'Can't they afford the Wing' I asked in a 'Why do *we* have to have him' tone of voice.

'Oh, he could go on the Wing all right, but he would have to have a Private Nurse and they can't run to that' she told me.

Before I could ask why he wasn't semi private she continued 'The reason he's on St. Vincent's is because he's on suicide watch'. Suffering Jezzis!

'Keep an eye on him, but I don't believe he will do anything silly' she said going off to dinner.

The welfare of this pampered streak of misery was in my hands. His bed was facing the landing so I had the advantage of having him under direct surveillance. The disadvantage was that having declined night sedation he also had me in his line of vision thereby ensuring I carried out of his petulant demands which ranged from telling me to hand him a glass of water, already within his reach, to informing me he was entitled to privacy so he wanted his curtains pulled. I responded to all his demands without a word, ignoring the curtain issue which I knew had been a running battle throughout the day. In defiance he got out of bed to pull them them himself. He was on Morphine p.r.n for for back pain from the sacrococcygeal tumours invading his spine. He already had difficulty walking and the likely outcome was the tumours would invade his spinal column leaving him paraplegic. His injection was long overdue but I didn't know whether this was an act of masochism, or to allow him the sadistic delight of tormenting me. Whatever the reason I was determined to brook no argument with him so when I got up to pull his curtains back I laid it on the line for him. I told him if he wanted to behave like a baby then by Christ I would treat him like one, and this would include an early morning bed bath. His eyes blazed with surprise and rage but when he met the conflagration in mine he turned his light off and turned over to sleep. Some time later he got up to go to the ward toilets. The Nursing Book said he must be accompanied but I decided to test the curse and let him go alone. Out of the corner of my eye I saw him hesitate waiting for me to get up and follow him. I ignored him so he shuffled off. He had two methods of committing suicide in the toilets, slashing his wrists, or opening the window in the adjacent bathroom and throwing himself out. I decided that both methods were a far cry from taking a few tablets in the comfort of his own home so awaited the outcome of my trust in Sr. Vincent's judgement. She returned from dinner to find me chewing my nails and Aidan still in the toilets.

'How long has he been in there' she asked calmly.

'Fifteen minutes' I responded tersely.

'Well let's hope its only constipation that's keeping him busy' she said drily handling her beads for comfort.

I had visions of seeing my name emblazoned in the Herald and Mail following the Inquest into his death 'Negligent Nurse allows suicidal patient to bleed to death said Coroner' or 'Patient dies from multiple fractures when Nurse ignores suicide warnings'. Before I cracked I heard the shuffle of slippers coming up the ward and out onto the landing. Neither of us turned to look at him.

'Can I have my injection now Sister' he asked politely.

When it had been administered I put down his back rest, arranged his pillows for sleep and picking up his chart I enquired professionally 'Bowels opened?' He just nodded and closed his eyes.

Chapter 42

The following night's handover mentioned that Aidan had seen a Psychiatrist and was no longer considered a suicide risk. No further information was forthcoming apart from the fact that he would be staying in for a week to complete his Radium treatment. A very subdued teenager was sitting up in bed. The most notable thing about this scene was the tidiness of the bed, locker top and bed table. On the previous night, all three, plus floor, had been littered with crisp bags, sweet papers, American comics and other detritus, with his counterpane rolled in a ball at the foot of the bed. At a time when a tidy ward was striven for, the day staff must have been tearing their hair out at the thought Matron doing one of her 'surprise' rounds. Initially we were quite busy on Elizabeth Ward with two patients confined to bed so I was dimming the lights before I got the chance to talk to him.
'Do you need anything' I asked him, a question I would never have asked the Mr. Hyde persona that occupied the bed the night before.
'No thank you Nurse' he said quietly turning off his angle poise.
Whoever this Psychiatrist was he was a miracle worker. Perhaps he should have a few sessions with Sr. B.!

In the quiet of the early hours with my body reaching its zombie state and my hearing at it's most acute I heard some muffled weeping. I went quietly along the line of beds but everybody was asleep. I stopped by Aidan's bed and I knew from the rate of his respirations he was feigning sleep. I pulled the stool from under the bed, sat down and waited. After several minutes and without opening his eyes he said quietly
'I'm going to die'.

'So am I' I said in smart response.

He looked at me in confusion.

'We're all going to die' I said trying to lighten the moment.

Over the next hour I discovered how much I had misjudged the lad. Based on his behaviour I had made judgemental assumptions about him, some due to my youth and inexperience, but mostly because I knew so little about what few rights young people had to information. In an effort to protect him his sisters had denied that the growth removed from his testicle was malignant, and had told him the pain in his spine from secondary growths was a recurrence of an earlier football injury. His GP and Consultants went along with this deception as they did on many occasions with adult patients, believing they had the Divine right to do what they considered to be in the best interests of their patients. It was only when Radium treatment was mentioned that common sense told him that what he had been told did not add up. This was the reason for his acting out and threatening suicide. The Psychiatrist on discovering this had insisted on a meeting with all concerned, so Adrian now knew he had cancer, and assumed he also had a death sentence. I knew that like everybody else, he needed time to get his head around planning for a limited life span; in fact, he needed to be encouraged to plan to live instead of waiting to die. When I tried to explain to him that all the patients on the ward were in the same boat tears came into his eyes again. Sr. Vincent came along at this point so I left her to console him as I went off to butter bread. She sat and talked quietly with him until it was time to do the injection round.

I half expected to find he had been discharged when I went on duty the following evening but there he was sitting at the table with the Ambulants learning to play cribbage. They appeared to have forgiven his initial appalling behaviour and were including him in their camaraderie. I learned during the handover that he would remain on the ward for the duration of his treatment. This now involved a daily session with the Psychiatrist to work through his anger with his sisters, because although he was a paragon of virtue as a patient he was giving his sisters hell when they visited. He was still awake after everybody else had settled for the night so I told him he could come and sit with me on the landing and test me on memorising the names of the theatre sets. Getting to know him I found he had no extended family, and no friends due to the over protectiveness of his sisters and the geographic distance of his home from his former school. He had never had a birthday party or been allowed to have friends in the house. His sisters anti social lifestyle hindered integration with neighbours, their only visitor being the elderly Parish Priest who came to dinner once a month. Aiden did well in exams but they had forbidden the school from allowing him to participle in games following a minor injury. So he was neither fish nor fowl, not bright enough to want to pursue further education, and too socially inept to cultivate friends when he no longer participated in games. Apart from his newly acquired Psychiatrist he had no support network, and had a deteriorating condition that I knew was going to put him in a wheel chair soon unless Radiotherapy gave him some remission. It didn't help that we were forbidden from discussing a patient's condition with them. That was the prerogative of his Consultant who's manner to date didn't indicate a willingness to embark on any free and frank exchange of information. Sr. Vincent's method of circumventing this was to give Aidan some articles to read, and encouraging him to formulate a list of questions he wanted answered. During the next week he began to regard the Ward as a haven, a place where he had lots of male company and who, because of his age and diagnosis, was basking in universal sympathy. It also helped him to live in a state of suspended animation, allowing him to give no thought to his condition. Having raged at his sisters for keeping him in the dark, he was now in a phase of total denial, turning his anger on anybody who suggested he was fit for discharge. But discharged he was, with me promising to visit him at home. I was dreading the visit because I was dealing for the first time with the terminal illness of somebody my own age.

I became morbidly obsessed with death and began reflecting on things I would want to do if I had a limited life span. Despite my flaky Karma I was not really a believer in reincarnation, or in my soul living forever, I was egotistical enough to want to be remembered, or at least to have the opportunity to fulfil some of my dreams, if not my destiny. I realised that unless I was prepared to rob a bank a round the world ticket was a non starter, so most of my journeying or pilgrimages would have to be vicarious and in the company of Belloc, Steinbeck, Böll or other travellers. José Julián Martí Peres hero of Cuban Independence advocated planting a tree, writing a book and having a son as memorials. The first I could do, the second I could start but having a child was not part of the scheme of things unless Gregory Peck was prepared to father it. Suicide was not on the cards because I knew I would never put the family through the scandal. Whatever the outcome I knew when I died my funeral was already paid for with Gran's penny policy with the Pru.

It was remembering Mag O'Neill on the feast of All Soul's that put things in perspective. She knew what was real and important in life. My fantasised plans were all about me, me, and me. Maggo's had been about the welfare of her family and children, and leaving happy memories for them, content to make do with a bottle of Knock water for herself if a Pilgrimage was not possible.

Other patients too had had very modest wishes, to live long enough to see the in the New Year, or walk up the aisle with a daughter; dress a child for First Communion, see lambing through, or gather in another harvest. Small modest wishes and it was painful to remember that in poor Maggo's case they had not been granted. However Paddy Joe Delaney, following my premature announcement of his death, had survived another eight months, to welcome his first grandson. I wondered if he had been compos mentis enough to appreciate his last rites. God rest the lot of them and their simple life's well lived.

~ NOVEMBER ~

Chapter 43

I had seldom been in the basement apart from escorting the odd patient to the Radiotherapy or X-Ray Departments or picking up medication from the Dispensary or a meal from the Kitchen, so the Out-Patient area was a new experience, and my introduction to a month with the She Devil. 7.50 a.m. the first Monday in November found me ready to meet my doom in an empty Out-Patient's Department. I was expecting Duffy and Sr. Bernardino to be there already so went from room to room but found no sign of them. Taking the quickest way up to Theatre on the ground floor, which was out the side door and up the front steps, I went off to find them. I went into the ante room, knowing better than to traverse theatre in my shoes but the place was deserted.
'Where were you told to go' said Sr. Josephine whom I met in the hall.
'Outpatients' I said.
'Well get yourself downstairs again and wait.
Taking the internal stairs this time I made my way back to Out-Patients.
'Late on your first morning Nurse' said the cold furious voice of Sr. Bernardino glancing at a large round clock on the waiting room wall which read 8.10 a.m.
The injustice of it scalded my soul but not my tongue. 'Sorry Sister' I responded meekly. 'You're with Staff Nurse Duffy to day so go and find her' she ordered.
Connie Duffy was racing around like a dervish.
'Redmond, bear with me' she said handing me a bundle of file dividers saying 'Out Patients Clinic'.

'Clinic starts at 9.00am so go and pull these records, put today's date and the name of the patient on the divider, and put the divider where the record was'. Giving me a list she told me

'Pull the records in this order so that the first patient's records are available for Riordan when he starts.

Reader, if you are ever in a position to employ a filing clerk make sure you choose one suffering from an obsessive compulsive disorder, or one who at least knows how to put Mac and Mc's in chronological order. I had found eleven out of the sixteen records by 8.45am; dividers already in place told me the records were out to the Out Patients Clinic.

'Probably waiting for discharge letters to be written' Duffy guessed. Try the House Officers room' she said pointing me in the direction of their Office.

Holy St Anthony! Two desks with records stacked in wire trays. No wonder Sr. Bernardino was riven with rage. I tried to see if there was any discernable system being used. It was pure guesswork when I discovered that the trays were related to dates of last attendance. I returned to Duffy with this information but minus records, however, she knew that three of the patients were on three monthly review, and I recognised the name of a patient who had recently been on St. Vincent's Ward so I managed to find another four records, fifteen out of sixteen was a good result I learned.

Records were only the first hurdle. While I was manically chasing them Duffy had been collecting X-rays, Pathology Tests and Histology Reports and then checking the records to ensure that all requested tests were available when the patient was seen. Patients began arriving by 8.30am. Despite having timed quarter hourly appointments they ignored this fact. Being used to General Hospital's block booking methods, which basically degenerated into a first come first seen service, they believed the earlier they came the earlier they would be seen. Duffy paused long enough to tell me 'For God's sake make sure the right one goes in when they are called. We don't want any more Sweeney incidents, do we' she said within Sr. Bernardino's ear shot. Deliberately I fancy since she flashed her eyebrows at me.

I was more concerned that the records I had pulled actual belonged to the patients sitting there, and hoped that Duffy had checked them out. I spent the morning escorting patients for x-rays and blood tests, chaperoning women being examined, resetting trolleys and as far as Sr. Bernardino was concerned, not once did I manage to be in the right place at the right time. I was caught in a Catch 22 situation. For every action, there is an equal and opposite criticism so if I was zooming around I must be unorganized and needed to prioritize, but if I paused for reflection, I was lazy and needed to be given more work to do.

It was only when I saw Duffy bringing in Mr. Riordan's coffee tray mid morning that I realised we hadn't had a tea break.

'You get an hour for lunch instead' she told me when I asked.

'What time does clinic finish' I enquired.

'It finishes when it finishes' she responded ambiguously.

I understood her enigmatical answer when 1.15 pm arrived and the last patient departed. I assumed we could also depart but was quickly disabused by Duffy. 'We wait until Riordan and his entourage of students leave, *then* clinic is over. I noted that Sr. Bernardino had long departed for her dinner. It was past 1.30pm by the time I made it to the dining room where Mary had been keeping my meal warm. Being Monday it was Shepherds pie, so no great damage was done in the reheating, and with a boat full of gravy I wolfed it down in an empty room. Much to my delight Mary put a much appreciated pot of tea on the table.

When I got back to Outpatients Duffy had the sterilizers on already boiling up instruments and syringes used throughout the morning. We then set to attaching all test results in chronological date order into the records with a treasury tag. She gathered up the x-rays for return to the X-ray Department and handed me the records. I assumed they were for refiling so I couldn't believe my ears when she told me to place them on the chair by the door in the House Officers Room.
'But the dividers will say they are still in clinic' I pointed out.
'Redmond, it's your first day so for God's sake don't make waves' she advised. 'You will find many things that could drive you insane in the next month, so just let it ride because you won't change anything' she told me.
I wondered why such a capable and efficient nurse put up with it. 'Let's get on with the work' she told me showing me how to clean all surfaces in the consulting and examination rooms and set them up the next clinic. She told me about the routine for the week which I jotted down.
Monday morn; Review Clinic / pm clean up and filing / theatre prep.
Tuesday morn; Theatre /p.m. cleaning
Wednesday morn; Clinic new patients / pm ditto
Thursday morn; theatre / p.m.cleaning/ or Ward relief
Friday morn; Skin Clinic new patients / pm Review patients
'If there are no theatre cases you should be sent to relieve on the wards but Her Majesty will probably find you something to do.
'Go and have your tea and meet me in theatre at 3.30 we have drums to autoclave for tomorrow.
Theatre autoclaves were much bigger than the ward ones. Compared to sterilizers which worked by boiling instruments for an hour or more, autoclaves could sterilize all kinds of equipment by subjecting it to high pressure saturated steam at 121 °C or

higher in 15–20 minutes, depending on the size of the load and the contents. As well as drums of dressings it could take trays of instruments plus green draping towels all wrapped in linen paper and deliver it to you like a steamed pudding in a guaranteed timescale. It could probably steam puddings as well but I resisted the temptation to try.

Chapter 44

As I went through the Anteroom doors to Theatre the following morning the words of the Mad Hatter came to mind "Beware the Jabberwock my child, with eyes aflame, jaws that bait, and claws that catch'. I went through to the large room containing the autoclaves, sterilizers and instrument washing sinks. There was a skinny woman in 'blue scrubs' and theatre cap over by the instrument sink. I thought it was Duffy and was about to ask where C.J. was when I realised it *was* C.J! Oh my God! This was priceless! Why hadn't any of the Probationers mentioned it before? Was I the only one stupid enough to think she scrubbed up wearing her seagull head dress and voluminous woollen habit? I was so riveted with fascination, and a hysterical urge to shriek with laughter, that I didn't take in what she was saying so she had to repeat it, which obviously irked her. Good start Redmond.

Duffy had gone through the basics of where everything was the previous afternoon. I had found out I was never going the find scrubs to fit me. All the trousers were too long with the waist up to my armpits. Duffy tightened the waist string around my ribs, hooked one end through the front of my bra, tied both strings in a bow and tucked the bow into my bra. This was a woman had never been subjected to Sr. Agnes's modesty regime! The scrub top came down nearly as far as my knees but a belt of one inch gauze bandage rectified that. A thing of beauty I was not but, at least I could function and keep my trousers up. She had also gone through uniform rules bringing back nostalgic memories of Donovan. Scrubs and clogs and no stockings were worn in theatre once you walked through the Anteroom into the changing room. If for any reason you had to go through the Anteroom back into the Hospital you had to do so in full uniform. A whole new Chapter of Bacteriology was opening up. I now had to worry about clean floors (clogs) dirty floors (shoes) clean rooms (scrubs) Hospital (uniform) when to wear a mask and when to go without, not to mention, who was sterile and who wasn't. I also had to learn scrubbing up rituals, but you don't, so I won't bore you.

The list of operations also went from clean to dirty, with the dirty one at the end of the list. On this list it was a colostomy, which would follow two patients for insertion of radium rods into their tongues. The first case of the day was the insertion of a paracentesis drain under local anaesthetic. Duffy had autoclaved the sets the day before, taking the now familiar instruments from their rows of glass cabinets. I felt guilty about not disclosing my acquired knowledge to her as she patiently went through the names and functions of the instruments she removed. Duffy scrubbed up for the first three ops while Sr. B supervised my 'running'. A misnomer if ever there was one since it was the only thing I didn't do. Although I had scrubbed my arms to the elbows with a sterile nail brush and carbolic soap until they were red raw I was 'unclean' in the sense that I was not allowed to touch anybody apart from tying the tags on their sterile gowns. Everything else I handled was with Cheadle forceps which stood in containers of Lysol at strategic points. If my clogs had not been a size too big for me I would have been quite the little moth dancing around the well illuminated table. As it was I had had to retrieve one of them with my foot from under Mr. Riordan's feet when he stepped back unexpectedly. I could feel Sr. Bernardino's eyes drilling holes in me.

'Ready for the rods now 'he said.

Sr. Bernardino pointed at the lead container that looked like a flask of tea. It was on an unsterile trolley, ergo, my brain told me it must be unsterile. However that was all my brain told me before it went into meltdown. I knew I couldn't support the weight of the flask to carry it with a forceps; neither could I deposit the flask among Duffy's sterile instruments. Before I could work out the logistics the Avenging Angel descended on me, and muttering imprecations she unscrewed the lid of the container and picking up a dressing forceps from its bed of alcohol she removed a sterile medicine glass from a covered dish on the trolley, and then manipulating the forceps removed a small rod from the container and dropped it into the glass. Clasping the glass with the forceps she deposited the rod on a piece of gauze on Duffy's tray telling me to close the flask again. I knew there was something very wrong with this procedure but didn't work it out until I had done it several times. The container was unsterile so I should have had to scrub my hands every time I touched it. I asked Duffy between ops about this anomaly.

'Normally there would be a runner just to deal with situations when you can't use a non touch technique, but in this instance we could never make a patients mouth a sterile environment so prevention of infection is the best we could hope for' she explained.

So began my Theatre experience. I have no idea why nurses would want to specialise in Theatre Nursing since there is little or no nursing involved. I found it technical, egotistical and elitist and suitable only for right handed practitioners. The only respite I got from Sr. Bernardino was when she was in the recovery room with the post op patients. To give her her due she joined us in the cleaning after lunch. The Armed Forces have a well worn joke 'If it moves salute it, if it stands still paint it'. In theatre the cleaning routine was

If you can see it clean it

If you can't see it clean it
If you can reach it clean it
If you can't reach it clean it
If it's made of stainless steel scrub it
If it is made from rubber, soak it
If it is used replace it
If it is not used recycle it

Walls, doors, floors, lights, trolleys, Boyle Anaesthetic machines, operating table, sinks, instruments, rubber tubes; every inch of theatre was cleaned with a liquids considered suitable for the job. The heady mixture of fumes from Alcohol, Carbolic, Ceepol, Lysol, Phenol and Savlon reminded me of Annie Lawlor and her fetish for Jeyes Fluid. Duffy and I ended the day cutting squares of gauze and making cotton wool balls to put in drums for autoclaving. I packed everything for sterilizing into two of the autoclaves and by the time they were 'cooked' Sr. Bernardino was back checking everything before locking up. I opened the autoclaves to discover to my horror that I had put the drums in without opening the perforated vents, so steam had not been able to permeate, hence sterilizing had not taken place. Sweet Heart of Jesus font of love and mercy, I was left with the dilemma of confessing, or pretending they were sterile and telling Duffy later. However I had visions of the Theatre being used in an emergency so opted for the former. I have often wondered if Sr. Bernardino died from one of her apoplectic rages, or is she is still alive giving hell to staff in a home for the ancient deranged.

Chapter 45

New Patient Clinic was very different from Mondays Review Clinic. At least there was no need to worry about lost records, X-rays or Pathology results. Patient's arrived with sealed, heavy duty brown envelopes from their referring Hospital Consultant. As I became familiar with this method of transferring records I was struck by the fact that none of the seals appeared to have been tampered with. I know that in similar circumstances mine would have been steamed open at the earliest opportunity. It was a long day for the patients and their escorts. Some would have already have spent the night in Dublin. The most welcome sight for them was the tea trolley manned by a couple of St. Vincent de Paul volunteers. Duffy tried to make the day as unhospital like as possible by putting the two rows of waiting room chairs into a circle so that people could talk to each other. Apparently this created a running battle with Sr. Bernardino. She wanted them in rows.
'Put those chairs back in rows' she ordered me.
This would have meant disturbing the patient's already seated.
'Why' I said, with what I hoped was a polite tone of enquiry in my voice.
The intonation seemed to have got lost in verbalization.
'They look tidier in rows' she said with a finality that should have brooked no argument.
I looked at Duffy busy putting patients at their ease and made no move to carry out her order. I saw the vein in her forehead begin to throb so to avoid a confrontation in front of the patient's I walked towards her with trepidation and said quietly

'Sorry Sister I don't think that's a good enough reason'. I must have closed my eyes in the expectation of the usual verbal onslaught because I became aware that she had vanished. It was too much to hope that it had been in a puff of smoke. I knew I was living on borrowed time. The words 'pray for us sinners now and the hour of our death' went dancing through my mind.

The morning passed with the patients been processed by us and clerked by Mr. Riordon's entourage of fourth year medical students under the supervision of the two housemen. The great man himself didn't arrive until 1.30pm. Patients were then seen at quarter hourly intervals. Some had already been given a diagnosis by a Regional Consultant and were here to discuss options, others were attending to have the diagnosis confirmed, in both cases I thought fifteen minutes a paltry amount of time to have with a Consultant. But in an era where the least a patient knew the better I suppose the appointment time was considered adequate. Duffy was brilliant with the patients who had lists of questions they had wanted to ask Riordon but hadn't. I left her to it while I cleaned all the rooms and put the chairs back in rows.

There was an afternoon theatre list the following day so Duffy and I spent the morning preparing. She said nothing about the chairs but I knew she was aware of my confrontation so I told her what happened. 'I'm sorry you had to be involved Redmond' she said eyes burning with fury that Sr. Bernardino had drawn me in to the running battle. To cheer her up I asked her to test me on the biggest hurdle I had to pass in the next three weeks; the instrument identification and function test. We were scraping the barrel on obsolete and esoteric instruments by the time Sr. Bernardino appeared. Sr. Vincent's coaching had been worth it. Not a single mistake or misidentification. Duffy was bowled over with surprise, as I hoped Sr. Bernardino would be when she signed my competencies. When I told Duffy how I achieved my expertise she just smiled and nodded in satisfaction, saying 'Well that'll be one in the eye for you know who'.

Chapter 46

Dr. Courtney's Friday Skin Clinics were a lot more impersonal, with new patients in the morning and reviews in the afternoon. Insular patients were sitting quietly in rows which must have warmed the heart of Sr. Bernardino. I should qualify that; everybody was sitting quietly in rows except Jarvis Vincente. My former tea maker on sighting me picked me up and whirled me round the waiting room. If I wasn't cursed no one but his fellow patients would have witnessed this, however out of the corner of my eye I saw an amused Dr. Courtney and an incensed Sr. Bernardino. looking on. I waited for her castigation at the end of clinic but she merely informed me I had Saturday off and was on St. Elizabeth Ward on Sunday. I didn't dare remind her that she owed me three hours study leave for the week. I never got a single hour the month I was answerable to her.

I don't expect you to have sympathy for the damned, unless you are one of the cursed yourself. Monday started off well with every record found. Much to my delight I saw that Fancy Finnerty was due for review and kept an eye out for him and his wife. I initially missed him because I wasn't expecting him to be in a wheelchair. When a familiar voice said 'How's the going today Nurse' I turned to see a smiling Fancy. I immediately bent forward to hug him trying to hide my concern at his gauntness. His wife Moira was a cheerful as ever but could not disguise the worry in her eyes. He was interested in catching up on the Ward news so I was imitating a CJ rant when Moira's eyes warned me that she was standing behind me. I knew by her stony faced glare that I would pay for my fun later.

Duffy, bless her, put the Finnerty's in my charge to collate tests, x-rays and records and see them through the procedure. Fancy was functioning on one lung now but the good news, having been reviewed by Mr. Riordon, was that current x-ray's showed no new build up of fluid. The once frightening apparatus attached to large sealed jars were no longer a mystery to me. The procedure for inserting a tube to drain fluid from a lung was called a thorocentesis, while one inserted into the abdominal perineal cavity for ascites resulting from liver failure was a paracentesis. Both procedures brought great, but short term relief, to patients.

The end of the month was on the horizon. I remembered Sr. Catherine's advice about keeping one step ahead of Beelzebub's Hoor by keeping out of her way, working conscientiously to avoid her wrath, and standing up to her if the either of the latter didn't succeed. Her advice to ask either Sr. Josephine or Sr. Vincent to be present at my assessment session I didn't follow, when I asked myself 'why' in retrospect I found it difficult to answer. I think it was a combination of conceit that I could deal with anything she threw at me, and a residual belief that she couldn't in good conscience give me a bad report. It would be seen in my Schedule of Training to be in complete contrast to the reports already in there. Duffy had been through the schedule with me so although I was buzzing with adrenaline I wasn't worried when Sr. Bernardino announced it was assessment day. She made me jump through hoops keeping the setting out of a sterile General Set for surgery until near the end, finishing with instrument identification. If she was impressed she never showed it, but I bet her dentist noticed a marked deterioration in her molars the amount of teeth grinding she did. She filled in the Proficient column with a series of ticks and told me coldly she would return my schedule when she had written her report. Hell would freeze over before I would ask her for it.

The next day a breathless Rita Carroll came down to Out Patients to warn me that Matron would be sending for me. When Grace Laing had written confirming our acceptance for General Training she had mentioned that she would be writing to Sr. Mary Joseph for information confirming the completion date of our training, our state of health and a recommendation as to our fitness for General Training. I had no reason to worry about any of that despite Sr. Bernardino's pending report, so shoes polished, seams straight, clean apron and unmodified cap found me outside her office by pre arrangement mid afternoon. I was prepared for the initial 'ignoring' ploy but I was totally floored by her cold measured ire. I looked at the picture of Our Lady of Perpetual Succour on the wall behind her silently asking it why some nuns were so full of rage, but Our Lady just gazed sorrowfully back at me. There was no invitation to sit so I stood with my hands behind my back hiding my clenched fists. With preconceived ideas about why I was there, and the likelihood of leaving without a reference, it it took me a few minutes to tune in to the bomb blast directed at me. Words like Heathen England, Protestant Hospital, East End slums, Jack the Ripper, Mafia gangs, Marauding Lascars, Opium Dens and Jewish sweatshops were all factors mentioned in my misguided choice of training venue. The only things she left out were Oliver Twist's Jago and White Slavers (unless that was what Marauding Lascars got up to?) which led me to believe that her source of reference was more likely to be the News of the World than Charles Dickens or Alfred Morrison.

Why hadn't I sought her advice and guidance? It was not too late. She would forgive my ingratitude and I could have a list of

Catholic Hospitals in England who would only be too happy to have me on her recommendation, and would even pay my fare. Would I consider it? I was just beginning to formulate an apology for not consulting her when she went one step too far.

'I would have thought that having been rescued from the tenements of Dublin you would be the last one to choose to take yourself off to the slums of East London, but then, as they say, you can take the girl out of the slum but not the slum out of the girl.'

Ten months earlier I had left her office in tears of rage. But now, I managed a broad smile and said cheerfully

'Sure you never spoke a truer word Matron; you're wise enough to know that you can never make a silk purse out of a sow's ear'. I was tempted to say it in the Dublineze vernacular but remembering Sr. Monica's hard work on my elocution I said it in my best Foxrock enunciation.

Exiting without permission I realised I hadn't answered her question, but I think she got the message. I wondered how many years another Jackeen would have to wait to be accepted for training. I warned Rita what she was in for, but with only days till she was back in Co. Monahan, and her mind firmly made up, we planned our reunion within the sound of Bow Bells. My destiny was set.

~ DECEMBER ~

Chapter 47

The excitement of Dubliner Ronny Delaney winning an Olympic Gold Medal on the first of December completely overshadowed my eighteenth birthday tea. I had by then received 'The List' from Grace Laing. A very modest list compared to the St. Anne's one. I would be expected to possess

1 pair of Clarks black lace up shoes / or
 Similar from any well known nursing range
3 pairs of black serviceable stockings
1 fob watch with second hand
1 pair of regulation nurse's scissors
2 drawstring laundry bags
3 dozen Cash's name tapes
£10 for text books and stationery
The latter can be set against salary and repaid at £2 per month.

As I sat at Gran's table the scene of the year before was recreated with me making a Christmas present list of replacement items, and ribald comments from Irene Fitz and Lena Breslin about the lack of underwear on the current list. Having spent most of the year in uniform my clothes were in good condition so apart from new underwear and a pair of shoes to be soled and heeled I was ready to go. There would be no shopping expeditions! To cut down on the expenditure on books I wrote off to Grace Laing asking for the names and authors of the text books, intending to see my lady with the birds nest hairdo. My return to the bookshop was a fruitful as before as she welded her magic rubber. My one regret was that I never got her name to write and thank her, but I have always remembered her with immense gratitude.

On my birthday itself I returned to the wards for my final month. Much to my delight I was on St. Vincent's with Mc Guinness and a new Probationer Mary Kenny from Monahan. It was Sr. Vincent's first day back on days; however she would be covering St. Peters because Sr. Josephine was rotating on to night duty. Dolly Mc Gee would be running the ward and I was now the most Senior Probationer in the Hospital! I could be trusted with the Medicine Cupboard key, preparing for ward rounds and escorting Matron on her 'surprise' visits. It was a few days before Sr. Vincent had time for a chat. 'Bring your Schedule with you' she said in passing. When I went to her office I went without it explaining that Sr. Bernardino had not returned it to me. 'Go and get it, tell her I want it *now*' she said emphasising the *now*. I found her, and without emphasising the *now* told her Sr. Vincent needed my Schedule. 'I haven't finished with it' she said walking off. I relayed this response to Sr. Vincent whose pallid skin took on a rosy hue. Writing and sealing a brief note (which I was tempted to steam open) she asked me to transmit it to her fellow religious. Nothing happened until the following day when Sr. Vincent appeared with my Schedule. She went through the competencies Sr. Bernardino had signed off, read the accompanying Report Page and handed it to me without comment. I read;

'I do not consider Nurse Redmond to a suitable person to be a nurse. While her theoretical and technical knowledge can not be faulted she has a surly and inflexible attitude towards authority and is incapable of accepting direction. Her work shows attention to detail, and she has good clinical skills, however she has no respect for hospital rules or the dignity of her profession. The latter is amply demonstrated by her over familiarity with male patients. In the circumstances I can not recommend her for General Training'.

Although I had been expecting a bad report it was still like a blow in the solar plexus. 'What do you want to do about it' she asked an edge of anger in her voice. 'Nothing' I said. 'You could take it to Matron' she said firmly. (I don't think so!). I had been looking at the report trying to will it away. 'I've changed my mind' I said re-reading the page in front of me. At the end of the Report space were the words *This report must be read to the student and her signature obtained certifying that she has seen the report.* Surely that should read 'by' and not 'to'? So far nobody had read a report 'to' me. But there it was in black and white that one important little word. 'I want her to read it to me' I said. Sr. Vincent looked at me in puzzlement. 'I want to hear her say the words, I explained. 'I want to see her her face when she reads what she has written' I went on.

'Redmond, you'll be the death of me' she said smiling. 'Do you want me to be there' she asked longingly?

'Only if you want to be' I said meaning it, I was prepared to do it alone. 'But you could set it up' I said.

'Nothing like the present' she said glancing at her fob watch and lifting the phone.

Several minutes later a granite hewn nun and a gurrier from Summerhill were sitting opposite each other in Sr. Vincent's Office. 'I believe you have some questions about your Report' she stated, preparing for intimidation, argument and justification. 'No, Sister I responded 'Not I'. 'Then why are we here' she said her voice rising and pale gimlet eyes searing me. I felt like emulating Shylock and saying, 'Because I want my pound of flesh' but I knew what I really wanted was blood and that I was unlikely to get a jot so merely handed her the Schedule and said to her

'It says at the bottom of my report that you must read it to me'.

'You want me to read it to you she said with incredulity, looking at me as if I should be sectioned.

I just nodded pointing out the words to her. I sat silently through several insults to my intellectual capabilities and inquiries into what words I did not understand. Eventually she read what she had written, still not believing that I would not question it, and that that was all I wanted. I signed and dated the Report and thanked her. I suspected my asserting my rights completely threw her. She was so used to frightening others into submission that my response took that power away from her. I couldn't have explained this at the time, or what I thought I had achieved, I just knew that it was important to me to face her down.

Revenge is a dish best served as humble pie.

I passed the Schedule to Sr. Vincent when she came back to her Office. 'What would you have done if she hadn't read it to you' she asked with curiosity.

'Oh, I'd have taken the bus out to Blackrock to see Mother Provincial' I said with determination.

'Holy Mother of God, don't let me ever annoy you Redmond' she said in awe.'

'Ah, well if you kill a Canon when you're eight there's nothing much left to fear' I told her raised eyebrows

Chapter 48

Advent was upon us and despite the spectre of death hovering at the gate the whole hospital was abuzz with plans and rehearsals. Most patients would go home, but for those staying it would be as memorable as we could make it. Only two wards would remain open; St. Vincent's and St. Elizabeth's, so any private or semi private patients admitted would have to slum it for a couple of days. Decorating the two Wards and the Out Patient Waiting room engendered huge competition between Sr. Apolline, Sr. Vincent and Sr. Bernardino although none of them would admit to such secular frivolity. Each would have a donated tree but otherwise the rest was up to the Sisters and staff. Boxes of old decorations were taken out of storage with scathing remarks about the eejits who had thought them worth saving. On St. Vincent's Ward we sought inspiration and spondulix. I had been to visit Aidan twice since his discharge and had found him very hard going. He was petulant with his sisters, and self pityingly boring to talk to, however his eyes lit up when I told him about the Ward decorating competition. Apparently he had aspirations to be a set designer and was beside himself with excitement at the thought of the blank canvas of a Ward.

'How much money do we have' he asked.

'£7.10s' I told him, noting the 'we'.

He repeated the sum, his voice raising two octaves in incredulity.

'Well probably a bit more with a few raffles' I said in a hopeful voice.

I left him sketching plans while I set about explaining the situation to Sr. Vincent.

'Can he get himself up here to discuss what he wants to do' she asked, body language clearly stating 'We're in it to win it'.

No sooner said than done. Apart from not taking up a bed Aidan was on the Ward morning till evening feverish with plans, and persuading his sisters to sell raffle tickets in the echelons of the Civil Service.

Also at a loose end was Jarvis Vincente. At his Out-Patient Review he had told me he was seeking to leave the Brotherhood and return to his family in Staffordshire. He was attending Out-Patients for ultraviolet treatment and was spending his afternoons on the Ward whiling away time with the current lot of Ambulants. What Aidan couldn't do physically Jarvis took on, out on his Norton foraging for pine cones, sea shells, holly, mistletoe, twigs, toilet roll tubes and sundry other items. Aidan's scheme involved a lot of green, red and white ribbon which we couldn't afford so armed with a packet of custard creams I went off to see Maggie in the sewing room.

I heard her before I saw her. Busy on her machine she looked up when I entered. Maggie wasn't one for small talk so I knew there was no need to plamas her, but I tried to get in a little potted history of Aidan and his plans to win the competition for Sr. Vincent. I think it was the latter that did it.

'Bring me a tin of red dye and a tin of green and I'll see what I can do'   Remembering a school days fiasco of dresses dyed motley shades of blue I insisted on knowing the specific shades wanted by the designer in chief before getting the money from Mc Gee to add to the expenditure of a tin of gold paint, a bottle of white window paste, lengths of crepe paper and glue. Maggie's efforts were stunning. She had shredded old sheets set aside for mending into long three inch strips and leaving some of them white she had dyed the rest green or red. Not only that but she zigzagged the length of each edge to stop it from fraying. It must have taken hours, and I suspect, it had been done in her spare time. I don't think her minion was as thorough about rinsing out the washing machine. All our underwear came back that Friday with a hint of pink.

As well as the competition, we, the Probationers, would be expected to put on a Christmas tableau on the Saturday afternoon before Christmas which fell on Saturday 22nd. This would be held in the Out-Patients Clinic with invitations to family, patients and visitors. The tableau was a series of scenes depicting the Christmas Story from the Annunciation, to the appearance of the Three Kings. Each scene would be interspersed with an appropriate Carol. 8pm to 9pm every evening we would rehearse in an unheated Out-Patients. There were no lines to be learned because the narrator would read them, so apart from one brief solo which nobody wanted to sing we were set to go. By custom and practice Sr. Josephine produced this seasonal offering, so imagine our horror when Sr. Bernardino with script and baton entered the room. As a group we became tone deaf, fell over ourselves, lost the ability to read and the Cork brigade became totally unintelligible. After half an hour we were wilting with sweat, and she had lost all control of the situation. She could shout, insult and glare to her hearts content but she was flogging dead horses.

The next night was nearly as bad but with Mc Guinness doing the narrating and Mary Kenny offering to play the Virgin Mary the scenes began to take shape. Other characters fell into place with some of us doubling up in minor roles. However there was no improvement in the singing. Two of the twelve were tone deaf and one sang in a key she could not sustain. I wondered why

there were no Staff Nurses participating so asked Dolly Mc Gee. She enlightened me by telling me
'We all have Christmas off'.
'What days do you actually have off' I asked suspecting an evasion.
'23rd to 27th' she admitted.
I told her of our dire situation but got no sympathy.
'If you think I going to submit to *that one* roaring at me for the next fortnight you've got another think coming' she said in a 'I don't want to hear any more about it voice'.
I knew she and Sheila Moran could hold a tune so went to Sheila to appeal to her better nature. The woman had a heart of stone.
'There's no point going on a begging mission' Marion Sherry told me and Kathleen Mc Guinness. 'We need some heavy artillery'.
'St. Jude' I asked caustically?
We were all lying on our beds with our feet up on the wall thinking of a solution.
'No someone nearer home' Mc Guinness responded drumming her nails against her teeth.
'Who is it that can make you feel so guilty that you would do anything to remain in her good books' she asked?
Sr. Josephine's intercession worked. The following evening Biddy Lynch, Sheila and Dolly had swollen our ranks and we began to sound like a choir. Duffy has escaped because she couldn't sing and Winnie Mc Whinnie wasn't there because she hadn't inflicted her on us. The latter came in to see if her 'powers of persuasion' had worked and nodded in satisfaction as we went through 'Once in David's City' with our two tone deaf colleagues miming. Dolly took on the solo and Mc Guinness carried on as narrator with me as understudy; she with her Waterford accent, me with my well enunciated Dublin one. Although nothing was

said nobody from Cork was suggested for the narration. While I had got used to the speed and cadence of the accent, for the uninitiated they may as well be speaking Serbo Croat. Rehearsals continued with Sr. Bernardino having little to do but direct, which she did civilly and quietly.

Chapter 49

Dolly prepared for her eight line solo as one would for a taxing aria from Wagner's Ring Cycle. We were sick of it, and more than fifty years on I can remember every word even though I've never heard it sung again. The Ward was being transformed. The tree was decorated, Maggie's streamers twisted in barleycorn spindles traversed the ceiling pinned in place with bunches of red and green balloons. Each of the five windows had artistic drifts of snow painted on the panes with white paste and each windowsill had a length of gamgee on which reposed a selection of holly and gold painted pine cones and twigs awaiting traditional red candles as centre pieces. With very little money left for tinsel, baubles and candles I suspected it would be folly to entrust it to the unworldly Jarvis. There was nothing for it but to offer to get them, and to grovel to The Gran.

We met up in Woolworth's tea room for her to take me shopping in Moore Street where the dealers had transformed their stalls into a fairyland of glitz and glitter and twinkling multicoloured Christmas lights.

It was not my intention to submit Jarvis Vincente to the culture shock of this experience but he had been entrusted with the money, and offered to carry all the shopping, and since this included six large swedes who was I to dissuade him? I therefore considered he deserved the Inquisition he endured while chewing his way through a piece of gur cake. It was brutal but he stood up well to it and once the Gran clarified that neither of us has any romantic notions about each other she lost interest. He was mightily impressed by her bargaining skills, admitting he could never have got a quarter of the amount of stuff we ended up with. I failed abysmally to get any sympathy from him when I disclosed my lifetime of traumatic shopping experiences.

'Sure she's a great character' he said smiling broadly. 'I think she's lovely'.

I was too young to appreciate what he was saying. I would have preferred a fairytale kind of granny who never embarrassed me, but then what kind of childhood would I have had if she had not managed to spread a meagre budget so prudently, and who could I call on now to best the dealers?

Life on the Ward went on with its expected sorrows. We had two deaths coming up to Christmas week, with a third one expected within days. It put our plans into perspective. We were going to make it the best Christmas ever for the patients who would be with us. I had felt relatively uncursed for weeks but then my luck ran out.

'I'm just popping over to my room' Mc Gee told me.

'No problem' I told her.

I could now handle anything, even Seamus Hickey from up behind God's back in the unforgiving wilderness that was Connemara. Nicknamed the Widow Maker by the other men because he seemed intent on blowing up the Ward by smoking in his oxygen tent he was in the last stages of Mesothelioma a legacy of his years asphalting the highways of England.

Anyway Sr. Vincent was downstairs so what could go wrong?

Well for a start Aidan chose this moment in time to knock over a pot of glue. He was working at the ward table and had moved some protective newspapers to make room for a cup of tea. The glue dribbled across the paper and on to the floor where the Ambulant with the tea trolley failed to notice it. Glue spread by the trolley wheels and the patient's slippers defaced the parquet floor as the rest of it stuck to the spread out newspaper and table.

While there were no commercial claims at that time that glue bonded instantly, the brown tar like mess, made from rendered animals, would soon become as brittle and hard to remove as Cleeve's toffee from the crevices in teeth. God bless the patient, a cabinet maker by trade whose quick thinking saved the floor.

'Big bucket of warm water and a bar of soap' he ordered pointing me in the direction of the sluice room.

Making foam he wiped and re wiped the floor with a tea towel and minimal wetting of the parquet. I made a start on the table by leaning across it trying to soak the paper off, and in doing so got half a page of small ads plastered across my bosom.

I suddenly realized you could hear a pin drop in the ward.

Matron had come to do a 'surprise' round.

She lasered me up and down as I walked towards her trying to ignore the antics of two wags behind her standing to attention in a mock Heil Hitler salute. I said nothing; she said nothing but indicated that I should proceed with the round. Sixteen beds later I had answered every question thrown at me. I waited for her at the Ward door to escort her to the Skin rooms but she had seen enough. Not a word of praise for my knowledge of the patients I was caring for. We parted with an admonition to straighten the bed wheels and to change my apron.

'A bit of Castor Oil now Nurse and that floor will be as good as new' my life saver told me gazing at my bosom and smiling.

It was only when I removed my apron that I realised that blazoned across my chest was the Charles Atlas advertisement 'You too can have a body like mine'.

Chapter 50

The morning of the 22nd dawned to a miserable cold drizzle and Mc Guinness moaning that she was dying. She got scant sympathy as we started on the mornings work. Gran and Annie Lawlor were supposed to be coming to the show but I thought, nay, hoped; the weather might put them off. However I soon had no time to worry about them as we organised Ambulants to take more chairs down to Out Patients, and then take charge of patients in wheel chairs that had no visitors to push them. I got dressed in my two backless theatre gowns, wearing one as intended, and the other with the opening in front to preserve my modesty. Bare foot, a length of cord around my middle, a tea towel on my head as a keffiyeh, and a stretchy hair band as an agal to keep the head dress in place and I made a passable Shepherd. The 'stage' was behind two opened out screens with the 'auditorium' a scant four feet away and there, in prime seats in the front row and dressed to kill, were Gert and Daisy personified.
'We got a lift' the Gran said nodding at two seagulls near the back.
Sr. Kevin and Sr. Francis had come. They were engrossed in conversation with Matron and I would have given my soul to have been a fly on the nearby wall. I saw Sr. Bernardino descending on me in a purposeful way, but before I could avoid her she had handed me a sheaf of paper.
'You'll have to do the narration' she said, 'Mc Guinness has gone down with the mumps'.
I silently cursed Kathleen into hell and out of it sparing not a thought for any discomfort she might be going through. At least

the narrator was more or less out of sight of the audience, sheltered in the gloom of the well lit tableaux. Cursed or not I could do this. Alas … When we had rehearsed the narration we had done so with the lights on, now, about to start the reading I realised I couldn't see a damned thing. The first line of Dolly's unaccompanied soaring prologue rang out flawlessly *'The Lord at first had Adam made out of the dust and clay'* and before I could do anything about my predicament Sr. Bernardino swept back the screens to begin the show. There was nothing for it but to amble across the Annunciation tableau in my shepherds garb to get the reflection from a spotlight directed on Helen Coffee playing the Archangel Gabriel. I could see by the look of consternation on her face that she was completely thrown. I could also feel Mary Kenny's eyes begging for an explanation as she knelt in her virginal blue. Their united sigh of relief was audible as I read *'And it came to pass that the Lord said Behold you shall conceive in thy womb and shall bring forth a son and you shall call his name Jesus;* .and the show got under way.

As the first carol was sung I dashed about like a headless chicken until I found a torch. I managed to narrate without incident to the end of the tableaux trying to avoid looking at the iridescent gleam of the kingfisher feather in Grans hat shimmering to her every approving nod. I could also see that Annie had her hankie out, but wasn't sure if it was to dab her emotion filled eyes, or to muffle her snuff infused sneezing.

Tea and biscuits were supplied for all, while we changed back into uniform and Sr. Marie invited everybody to vote on the best decorations. It was lovely to see my two referees who informed me that Matron had told them I was a credit to their school, and that if they wanted to recommend any other students of my calibre she would be happy to interview them. Now either

Reverent Mother was a better actress than Maureen Potter, or she had committed a massive mortal sin and should be on her way to confession.

Sr. Kevin collared Sr. Bernardino in passing telling me she had been her mentor during her Noviciate. I could see alarm rising in the latter's eyes waiting for further personal disclosures.
'We're so proud of her' Sr. Francis beamed, looking at me,
'Don't you think she'll make a grand nurse?
I looked at Sr. Bernardino but she was practicing *Custody of the Eyes*..
"Oh I'm sure she'll go far' she murmured weakly.
'Remind me to show you my Schedule of Training before you go' I told them and I saw the colour suffusing my adversary's turkey cock neck.
Revenge at last!
However, because I considered I'd already had my pound of flesh, I didn't shop her, but she wasn't to know that.

Voting slips in hand Gert and Daisy had set off with Jarvis on a tour of the Wards. The results wouldn't be known until Christmas Eve but I knew St. Vincent's Ward had those two votes in the bag. Aidan was there basking in praise and thanking Gran for her help. Seeing her looking at Maggie's streamers he made the mistake of asking her what she thought.
'They'd look a damn sight better if you'd starched them' she said without mercy.
The Oracle had spoken so Jarvis was up and down the ladder all the next day, Maggie put the starched streamers through the roller iron, and when Jarvis had re hung them they did look a lot better, but definitely not worth the hassle and disruption involved.

Chapter 51

With only twenty or so patients staying in for Christmas, and the Staff Nurses off, all Probationers would be on duty Christmas Eve and Christmas Day. Sr. Vincent had ensured I had St. Stephen's Day off with a late start on the 27th. Before the Wards filled up again most of the other Probationers would benefit from being able to go home for the New Year, but my last day on the Wards was New Years Eve. Jarvis had already departed to spend Christmas with his family but it looked as if Aidan was intend on spending his on the Ward. This seemed very unfair on his sisters since it was highly unlikely that he would even see another spring let alone another Yuletide. After some discussion with Sr. Vincent they agreed to let him stay in overnight to have Christmas Day on the Ward. His absolute delight when the Ward was chosen the best decorated was touching, but I knew that he had been able to put aside thoughts of his weakening state for far too long and that there was bound to be repercussions. Decorating the ward had sustained him, as had the camaraderie of the other patients. However he would no longer be able to spend his days there because it was becoming obvious that he needed bed rest, and not the make do of the easy chair he had managed to rest in up to now. He had also failed to keep his Psychiatric appointments so Sr. Vincent's plan was for everybody to face the problem in the New Year.

As soon as it got dark on Christmas Eve the lights were dimmed, the tree lights were switched on and bedecked red candles on the window sills, snug in their golden scooped out swede holders pierced with evergreens, were lit to illuminate the Ward. All the staff assembled down in the hall for a Carol Service. Turning our cloaks inside out to show the scarlet lining and holding lamps we ascended the stairs singing. Followed by our flock of seagulls we went slowly around St Elizabeth Ward then across the landing to St. Vincent's Ward ending up doing an ensemble on the landing. I tried not to look at the patients who had been moved to tears, as I had an overwhelming urge to join them. Following tea and Christmas cake, courtesy of Johnson, Mooney and O'Brien, Sr. Marie stood in for Father Christmas, dispersing a present for each patient from underneath the trees. I knew what was in each gaudily wrapped parcel because she had uprooted Marion Sherry and I from the sitting room during our off duty time to wrap them. Men blue wrapping - handkerchiefs, men red wrapping - socks, women pink wrapping – handkerchiefs, women yellow wrapping - soap and face flannel. I knew that over in the Nurses Home we would each find two presents under the tree. One would contain a pair of black stockings from Sr. Agnes, the other a present from one of the other Probationers. We had all drawn a name, and had secretly bought a *Christkind* present for that person, spending no more than 2s. 6d. As soon as I opened mine, disclosing a jar of lurid pink bath crystals I knew who it was from, because the synthetic smell of Ashes of Roses had wafted from Mc Guinness's wardrobe for days. She was not there to accept my effusive thanks. Her parents had taken her home to nurse her through her mumps. This gave me the opportunity to rewrap the jar and give them to a genuinely delighted Mary.

Christmas morning started with a fast. No breakfast until everybody had received communion. Mass would be said in the Chapel at 8.00 a.m. with the Priest coming in procession to the two Wards to give communion to the bed bound. The procession consisted of Sr. Marie ringing the small offertory bell followed by four young alter boys from the local Parish, one carrying the

Pascal candle, the second the smoking thurible, the third the boat full of incense and the fourth the asperonium of Holy Water and sprinkling brush. The vestment clad Priest in gold and white followed carrying the covered chalice. The Widow Maker was now out of his tent having oxygen by mask. While communion was being distributed over on St. Elizabeth Ward Sr. Vincent lit the candles on the cloth covered table which was now a converted alter with crucifix and wintergreens, and I scanned the Ward.

No sign of Hickey.

I made for the lavatories and following the gut wrenching coughing and the smell of Senior Service found him, purple faced, sitting on the toilet with his pyjama bottoms around his feet.

'Can't a man even have a crapeen in peace' he blustered as I marched him back to his bed.

Although most of the patients had very little appetite a full Christmas dinner was served, the turkey being carved by Mr Riordan. Mc Guinness, Kenny and I devoured the left over's in the Ward kitchen and could only pick at our own Christmas dinner served an hour later. Although it should have been one of the saddest Christmas's ever I felt cheered and uplifted and wished I had a magic wand that would give all these good people back their health. We had all worked a twelve hour day, so it had been my intention to make for home as soon as I got off duty, but when I got over to the Nurse's Home the sound of music and laughter attracted me. Some benefactor had donated a gramaphone and records specifically for our use, and with the chairs pushed back in the sitting room everybody was dancing. Marion Sherry grabbed me and despite protestations that I was a useless dancer soon had me whirling around the floor in a grip I would never have allowed a man to use. She held me so close that I could anticipate her every step and I felt exhilarated by my expertise. I regretted never having gone dancing during the year and promised to go the coming Friday.

Chapter 52

St. Stephen's Day and back at the Gran's I was eating left over Christmas goose, decapitated by Aunt May before its journey in the guards van from Oranmore to Kingsbridge. I spent the afternoon there it being open house for neighbours who came and went drinking gallons of tea, eating slices of Christmas pudding and cake, and indulging in Madeira Wine and hot toddies made from Annie's Baby Powers to keep the cold at bay, With the wind whistling as usual through her flat across the landing the latter was a necessity. She was delighted with the twist of Empire Mixture snuff I had bought her, but I knew what the Gran's reaction would be to her new kid gloves because it never varied. Annie winked at me and I tried not to laugh as she held up three fingers.

'Ah, youze shouldn't have', the Gran said on cue 'How much were they' and 'Can I take them back followed as night does the day.

As I got ready for Sheila's annual soiree that evening, the family's social event of the year, I realised this would be my last opportunity to say goodbye to most of them. Christy had generously bought my ticket to London, which included the luxury of a berth in a four birth cabin so I was all set to go providing I was not incubating Kathleen Mc Guinness's mumps. I thought it highly unlikely having succumbed to every infectious disease in my unimmunised childhood, while never missing a days schooling, but being cursed I was prepared for the worst.

Back on duty the following day, with a head still pounding from unaccustomed alcohol one of the Ambulants came up to me to tell me the tea he had poured for Hickey was getting cold. No sign of Hickey so I went to the toilets and there he was, as before, but now ashen faced, a smouldering cigarette butt still attached to the corner of his lower lip, ash dribbling down his chest and having already made Mrs. Hickey a widow. I called for Kenny to go and get Sr. Vincent and removing Sr. Josephine's card from the back of my notepad I began the prayer for the dying. My mind went back to the start of my training when I was first given the card, and my petrified state at the thought of having to use it. I remembered my pre-emptive use on Paddy Joe Delaney, but I had experienced enough death by now to know not to worry about a resurrection for Seamus Hickey.

I have never checked out Donovan's belief that I could claim a Plenary Indulgence.

The 1s/6d dance at the Chrystal Ballroom the following evening was a total and utter disaster. Girls congregated on one side of the Dance Hall with a mixture of unprepossessing sweaty, damp handed males on the other. I tried not to catch anybody's eye, already regretting my decision to come. Sherry and Coffee were swept away within seconds of entering the 'showing ring' then somebody politely asked me to dance. He looked clean, sounded nervous and was quite decent looking. Our difficulty started in the hold. Initially I thought he must be left handed or something but then he cannoned into me again and again until we had to come off the floor.

'What's wrong with you' I asked him.

'There's nothing wrong with *me*' he said nursing his bruised toes.

'Why do you insist on leading' he asked in puzzlement.

I looked at the other dancers gliding around in harmony, and if Marion Sherry hadn't been on the other side of the floor I'd have cheerfully reefed her beehive hairdo from its roots. The mortifying fact was she had taught me to dance in the lead position, and I hadn't known any better. My, would be, dance partner bought me lemonade while I explained my predicament.

'Ok you can lead' he told me, but with him being at least 6" taller it didn't work. It also didn't help that neither of us could stop laughing. I released him to find himself another partner and I was well and truly tucked up in my bed by curfew.

The last day of the old year coincided with the end of my training contract so I spent most of it saying my goodbyes. I sought out Maggie first, to thank her for ensuring I looked like a nurse and not a Victorian orphan, and for all her other help, then Duffy for teaching me real nursing and sustaining me through my month with the She Devil, and Mary who saved me several times from ending up on Sr. Agnes's hit list by getting me out of bed at 6.45am on cold frosty mornings. Aidan had not appeared for several days so I left a letter for him because I knew I would be out of my depth bidding him farewell at home. I then went down to the Chapel to have a last look through the names in Book of Remembrance. Nearly one a week for the previous year, seventeen of whom I had nursed to their final breath.

Back on the Ward Sr. Vincent handed over my Schedule of Nursing.

'Do you want me to read your final report' she asked mockingly. I just smiled and looked at the page. My eyes were swimming with tears as I finished it, noting that it had been signed by Sr. Josephine and Sr. Apolline as well. It read

Nurse Redmond has completed her training and has satisfactorily acquired the competencies set out in her Schedule of Training. She has the makings of an excellent nurse, with very good interpersonal skills. Her nursing o terminally ill patient's has been undertaken with kindness and compassion. She is a competent and safe practitioner, demonstrating a cool head and calm attitude in crisis situations. Her nursing care of all patients has been beyond reproach, as has been her support to her colleagues. Her attitude to those in authority has always been respectful and flexible. We would highly recommend her for General Training.

I spent the rest of the day bursting into tears at the slightest provocation. I would like to be able to say that I sought out Sr. Bernardino and Matron to say 'Goodbye' but I didn't. I wasn't that much of a masochist nor did I have that much generosity of spirit.

The New Year was heralded in in a City of churches with a cacophony of bells, Liffey foghorns, factory whistles and a curfew extended for those who wanted to see in a New Year. As for me, having requested my suitcase from the basement I was packed and ready for bed by midnight. The following morning Christy was in the driveway waiting to load my suitcase as Sr. Agnes saw me off. A week later he was unloading the same suitcase at the gangplank of the 'Hibernia' B&I Ferry. In the darkness of a moonless evening the boat left the shelter of Dun Laoghaire harbour, and as the lights along Dublin Bay receded the first surge of the Irish Sea caught the bow. Co-ordinates were set for the crossing and as the vessel adjusted its trim I headed for Holyhead and exile.

~ ~ ~ ~ ~ ~

OTHER MEMOIRS BY

Bernadette M Redmond

I DREAMT I DWELT IN MARBLE HALLS

THE SUMMER CHILDREN

PEA SOUP AND JELLIED EELS

A PROMISE OF TOMORROWS

~ *PEA SOUP AND JELLIED EELS* ~
~ JANUARY 1957 ~

Chapter 1 Circling the Drain

Following my journey across the Irish Sea on the B&I Ferry, the Hibernia, and a six hour journey on the Holyhead to Euston Mail Train I sat stupefied with tiredness in the tube longing for a peaceful death. I had been met at the barrier by a dumpy, sullen, monosyllabic student nurse, who had been picked on by an all powerful Home Sister to meet the train and deliver me in one piece to her office. Overawed and apprehensive I followed her meekly down into the bowels of the earth taking a seat beside her on the Circle Line Tube. I expected my first Underground journey to Bromley-by-Bow to be brief and uneventful and estimated that a further 15 minutes travel wouldn't kill me.

'Seven stops to Tower Hill' she volunteered. I nodded, too tired to talk. I fell to reading the strip of advertising panels above the heads of the passengers opposite me. Interspersed by maps of the route and 'No Spitting' signs I learned that;

'Rip Van Winkle fell asleep
It was a longish snooze
His clothes indeed were sadly worn but not his Rebuilt Shoes'.

~

'No home remedy or quack doctor ever cured syphilis or gonorrhoea.
Seek free confidential advice at the Middlesex Clinic'.

~

North, South, East or West, Fry's Cocoa is the best'.

'Don't be a Fool do Littlewoods Pools'

Eventually my eyes drifted up to the route map opposite just as we came in to Notting Hill Station.
There was definitely something wrong here.
 The Circle line was built to join up the main railway termini and had 27 stations on its circular route and was the favourite line, and home-from-home for twenty hours a day of the homeless and dispossessed. Most of its route, and all of the stations, are shared by either the District, Hammersmith, City and Metropolitan lines so getting off at Tower Hill and hopping on the District Line to take us further East we should by now have been alighting at Bromley-by-Bow.
'We're going the wrong way round' I told my surly companion whose head was buried in a 'Woman's Own' she had found abandoned on an empty seat. If she had said anything besides 'Oh crumbs' I might have considered forgiving her but my prolonged muttered blasphemous response would have had my Guardian Angel shocked to the core and kept a priest busy for a week deciding on a penance. I later learned it was her day off and that she had not been a willing volunteer.
 I had chosen to train at St. Andrews Hospital E3 as a result of a recruitment drive by English hospital Matrons who were in Dublin seeking girls willing to train as State Registered Nurses. I knew that if I applied to any Irish Hospital to do my General Training I would have to pay £200 for the privilege. In the United Kingdom I would be trained free *and* get a salary. Coming to the end of a year's pre training course at St. Anne's Skin and Cancer Hospital I was persuaded by a fellow nurse, Rita Carroll to accompany her to various Dublin hotel lounges to let the

Matrons give us the once over. Armed with our training Schedules we presented ourselves for interrogation and scrutiny while consuming the coffee and biscuits provided at each venue. All four Matrons we saw offered us a place 'subject to completion of our course and acceptance by their hospital's Board of Governors', the latter I knew was a mere formality if Matron had given us the nod. It was gratifying and a huge relief to realise our General training was assured. Our futures could be in Birmingham, Liverpool, London or Manchester. Both Rita and I had been very taken by Grace Laing, the Matron from St. Andrew's in London's East End. Sitting with her and three other possible recruits in Wynn's Hotel I felt she was the only one who had shown a genuine interest in our individual backgrounds and reasons for emigrating. It was also reassuring to be told that she had several ex Probationers from St.Anne's in training and that half of her trained staff was Irish, so Carroll and I both registered an interest in joining the 1957 January set.

What we didn't know at the time was that a goodly proportion of the Sisters appointed before her tenure were less than happy with her views on improving the Hospital regime and Nurse Training, and of foraging for potential recruits in Ireland and the Dominions. Nearer home her tendency to choose candidates with character and potential meant giving opportunities to girls who had had to leave school without formal qualifications due to the drudgery of family duties. She had to get the Board of Governors on side to do so but since her choices proved their worth she usually got her way.

What I *did* know was that I was part of a generation whose future would be on a foreign shore. Ireland, an impoverished country with a dismal economic environment and De Valera's deeply conservative theocratic government would not be able to meet either our aspirations or expectations in the furtherance of a career. Our exodus was rationalized by many families as a temporary expedient until things improved at home but I was realistic enough to know that my exile would be a long one.

Made in the USA
Charleston, SC
10 December 2013